W9-ARO-470

# EYEWITNESS
# WORLD WAR II

Grainger:
I cherisH You So much and a day
doesn't go By That I don't think of you!
Jim So glad you aRe a History Buff, That's
Knowlege that will Be with you all of Your
life
      Know I Love You So much -
            forever
            NaNa
                  chrestmas 2022

German Biber

A child's "Mickey Mouse" gas mask

Star of David badge

National emblem of Hitler's Germany

US Strategic Air Forces sleeve badge

Symbol of the Vichy State of France, 1940–44

Japanese naval sextant

Moaning Minnie

# EYEWITNESS

# WORLD WAR II

Polish medal

Russian medal

AUTHOR **SIMON ADAMS**
PHOTOGRAPHER **ANDY CRAWFORD**

Soviet T-34 tank

**DK**

IN ASSOCIATION WITH
THE IMPERIAL WAR MUSEUM

Camp currency

German Enigma
cipher

Binoculars

# DK | Penguin Random House

## REVISED EDITION

### DK LONDON

**Senior Editor** Carron Brown
**Senior Art Editor** Lynne Moulding
**US Editor** Megan Douglass
**US Executive Editor** Lori Cates Hand
**Managing Editor** Francesca Baines
**Managing Art Editor** Philip Letsu
**Production Editor** George Nimmo
**Production Controller** Samantha Cross
**Jacket Design Development Manager** Sophia MTT
**Publisher** Andrew Macintyre
**Associate Publishing Director** Liz Wheeler
**Art Director** Karen Self
**Publishing Director** Jonathan Metcalf

**Consultant** Philip Parker

### DK DELHI

**Senior Editor** Shatarupa Chaudhuri
**Senior Art Editor** Vikas Chauhan
**Art Editor** Sifat Fatima
**Assistant Editor** Sai Prasanna
**Project Picture Researcher** Aditya Katyal
**Managing Editor** Kingshuk Ghoshal
**Managing Art Editor** Govind Mittal
**Senior DTP Designer** Neeraj Bhatia
**DTP Designer** Pawan Kumar
**Jacket Designer** Juhi Sheth

### FIRST EDITION

**Project Editor** Melanie Halton
**Senior Art Editor** Jane Tetzlaff
**Art Editor** Ann Cannings
**Assistant Editor** Jayne Miller
**Managing Editor** Sue Grabham
**Senior Managing Art Editor** Julia Harris
**Additional photography** Steve Gorton
**Production** Kate Oliver
**Picture Research** Mollie Gillard
**Senior DTP Designer** Andrew O'Brien

This Eyewitness ® Guide has been conceived by
Dorling Kindersley Limited and Editions Gallimard

This American edition, 2021
First American edition, 2000
Published in the United States by DK Publishing
1450 Broadway, Suite 801, New York, NY 10018

Copyright © 2000, 2004, 2007, 2014, 2021
Dorling Kindersley Limited
DK, a Division of Penguin Random House LLC
22 23 24 25 10 9 8 7 6 5 4 3
004–314469–Aug/2021

All rights reserved.
Without limiting the rights under the copyright reserved above,
no part of this publication may be reproduced, stored in or introduced
into a retrieval system, or transmitted, in any form, or by any means
(electronic, mechanical, photocopying, recording, or otherwise),
without the prior written permission of the copyright owner.
Published in Great Britain by Dorling Kindersley Limited

A catalog record for this book is available from the Library of Congress.
ISBN: 978-0-7440-3904-7 (Paperback)
ISBN: 978-0-7440-2898-0 (ALB)

DK books are available at special discounts when purchased in bulk
for sales promotions, premiums, fund-raising, or educational use.
For details, contact: DK Publishing Special Markets,
1450 Broadway, Suite 801, New York, NY 10018
SpecialSales@dk.com

Printed and bound in UAE

## For the curious
**www.dk.com**

MIX
Paper from
responsible sources
FSC™ C018179

This book was made with Forest Stewardship Council™ certified
paper—one small step in DK's commitment to a sustainable future.
For more information go to www.dk.com/our-green-pledge

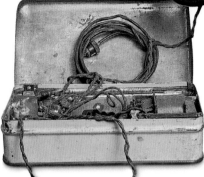

Homemade wireless
receiver used by a
Dutch family during
the occupation

British fire service
badge

Straw snow boots
made by German
soldiers in Russia

Japanese prayer flag

# Contents

Camp food
parcel

# A world divided

After World War I, the world was split into three main camps: democratic nations—including Britain, France, the Netherlands, Czechoslovakia, Belgium, and the US—where people elected their governments; nations ruled by dictators, including fascist Italy, Nazi Germany, and nationalist Japan; and the communist state—the Soviet Union (USSR)—meant to be run by workers but really run by the tyrannical Josef Stalin. Conflicts between these three camps led to a world war in 1939.

*Blue-bordered royal coat of arms*

### Italian fascism

Italian fascists used the fasces (an ancient Rome symbol of power) as their symbol. But Italy remained a kingdom, so its flag bore the royal coat of arms.

### Spread of fascism

In 1922, Benito Mussolini turned Italy into a fascist (dictator-led) state. By the 1930s, fascist rulers ran Spain, Portugal, Austria, Romania, and Germany—where the Nazi Party took fascist ideas to the extreme.

*Stainless steel figures are young, strong, and attractive*

*Hammer*

*Sickle*

### Soviet symbol

The hammer (for industrial workers) and sickle (for farm workers) was the Soviet Union's symbol and was on the national flag.

*Vera Mukhina's Worker and Peasant statue, for the Paris World's Fair, 1937*

### Power to workers

Communists, who were against private ownership, took power in Russia in 1917 and formed the Soviet Union. Few countries trusted it or its leader, and refused to support Soviet beliefs.

*Soldiers carrying NSDAP (Nazi Party) swastika banners*

## The Nazi Party

Set up in 1920 and led by Adolf Hitler, the National Socialist German Worker's (Nazi) Party believed blond, white Germans were a master race. The Nazis regularly held vast rallies, where members paraded with banners and listened to speeches from Hitler and other leading Nazis. When the Nazi Party came to power in Germany in 1933, they held a rally every year (shown here) in Nuremberg, south Germany, showing their strength, determination, and Hitler's power over his party.

## Imperial Japan

Japan fought on the side of Britain, France, and the US in World War I, but felt cheated when given little new territory. In the 1920s, nationalists came to rule Japan, wanting to make it an imperial power in Asia.

*Imperial Japanese army uniform, c. 1930s*

> "After 15 years of despair, a great **people is back on its feet.**"
> —Adolf Hitler, 1933

## Nazi symbol

The swastika is an ancient religious symbol, common in Greece and India. Adolf Hitler adopted the swastika as the symbol for the Nazi Party, and it appeared on the German national flag in 1935.

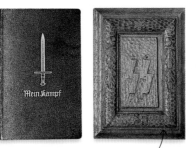

*Presentation box for a copy of* Mein Kampf

## Hitler's manifesto

Hitler wrote *Mein Kampf* (*My Struggle*) in 1924. It was ignored at the time, but clearly stated what he intended to do if he won power, such as creating a large army and persecuting Jewish people.

## The Reichstag fire

An arson attack on the Reichstag (parliament) building in Berlin on February 27, 1933, paved the way for the rise of the Nazi rule. Hitler alleged that the communists wanted to topple the government and used this false charge to take absolute control of Germany.

*Reichstag fire on February 27, 1933*

## Treaty of Versailles

After its defeat in World War I, Germany was forced to sign a treaty in 1919. It lost its empire and was banned from having a large army. Most Germans supported Hitler's refusal to accept these terms.

# Heading to war

In 1933, Hitler's Nazi Party came to power in Germany and began to build its army. In 1936, Hitler sent troops to the Rhineland—a German industrial area next to France and Belgium—then took over Austria and parts of Czechoslovakia. Meanwhile, Italy invaded Albania, Greece, and North Africa, and Japan invaded China. Strong ties grew between Germany, Italy, and Japan. By the late 1930s, Britain and France were reequipping their armies, while the US watched Japan's rise with concern. The world was preparing for war.

## Japan invades China

After taking over the Chinese province of Manchuria in 1932, Japan launched a full-scale invasion of China in 1937, seizing the capital, Nanjing, and much of the coast.

### Events in North Africa

Italy's leader, Mussolini, wanted to build a new Roman Empire in North Africa and turn the Mediterranean into an "Italian lake." Italy invaded Abyssinia (now Ethiopia) in 1935, sending emperor Haile Selassie, right, into exile.

## Nazi–Soviet pact

On August 23, 1939, the Soviets and German foreign ministers signed a nonaggression pact, which left Germany free to invade Poland and western Europe. They met again to confirm the division of Poland between them.

*Soldiers destroy the border barrier between Poland and German-controlled Danzig*

## Dictators unite

Italy's leader Mussolini (left) was at first hostile to Hitler (right) because Hitler wanted to invade Austria, Italy's neighbor. Gradually, the countries drew closer and formed a partnership in 1936, the Rome–Berlin Axis, which later included Japan and other countries. In 1939, Germany and Italy signed a formal alliance, the Pact of Steel, and fought together early in the war.

## Hitler moves into Austria

In March 1938, Hitler took his troops into Austria and declared an Anschluss (union) between the countries, breaking the Treaty of Versailles. Most Austrians favored the union, but nearby countries were concerned at Hitler's growing power.

## Britain and France together

This 1938 visit of King George VI (far left) and Queen Elizabeth to France marked Britain and France's close ties. They were alarmed by Germany and Italy's growing strength and, in 1939, agreed to help Poland, Romania, and Greece if Germany or Italy attacked.

## A peaceful approach

In 1938, European leaders agreed to placate Hitler and signed the Munich Agreement. This let Germans in the Sudeten area of Czechoslovakia unite with Germany. British Prime Minister Neville Chamberlain (above) said it guaranteed peace. Six months later, Hitler took over all Czechoslovakia.

**German forces invading Poland**

## Invasion of Poland

Hitler demanded the Polish Corridor— a strip of Poland dividing East Prussia from the rest of Germany. Poland resisted, so he took it; German forces here are seen dismantling the border posts in 1939 as they invade Poland. In response, Britain and France declared war on Germany—World War II began.

# Preparing
# for the worst

War loomed in 1938–1939, so Britain, France, Italy, and Germany prepared for the worst, with plans to ration food and raw materials. France had already built the Maginot Line to defend it from German invasion. Britain expected its major cities to be bombed soon, so took care to protect its people, digging shelters and issuing gas masks. Once war broke out in September 1939, children were evacuated to the countryside, but it was the German invasions of April–May 1940 that really tested these precautions.

### Guarding the home front

Toward the end of the war, German men aged 16–60 not already in the army were called to the Volkssturm (home guard). They had little training and had to make do with what weapons they could find.

Troops and weapons are transported on the Maginot underground railroad

### French defense

The Maginot Line, France's main fortification, took six years to construct (1929–1934) and stretched along France's eastern border with Germany. It consisted of antitank defenses, bombproof artillery shelters, and forts, many linked by underground railroads.

**German gas mask**

Grenade made from a wine bottle

### Gas masks

Everyone in Britain was issued with a gas mask. In Germany, only those considered high risk, such as children, air-raid wardens, and Nazi Party officials, were given masks. Gas was never used by either side, so the masks were never needed.

**Tin-can mortar bomb**

### Improvising

The British Home Guard was a voluntary unit that protected defense installations and watched out for enemy infiltration. They had few weapons and so they improvised, using cans to make mortar bombs and bottles for grenades.

S.Filtereinsatz für den zivilen Luftsch...
...tei gegen alle chemischen Kampfstoffe sowie gegen saure Ga...
...d gegen Schwebstoffe (Nebel und Rauche) Schützt nicht ge...

Gas filter

## Air-raid shelters

Most British city-dwellers installed an underground Anderson shelter (corrugated-iron tunnel) in their yards. In February 1941, there were Morrison shelters (steel cages for use indoors) for those without yards.

## Balloon protection

Large barrage balloons protected Britain's cities from air raids. They were launched before a raid and trailed steel cables beneath them. Bombers had to fly high to avoid the cables, reducing their accuracy.

## "The enemy sees your light! Make it dark!"

This German poster warns civilians to keep all lights shielded at night or risk helping enemy bombers to find their town. Blackouts were compulsory throughout Germany and Britain.

👁 **EYEWITNESS**

### German rationing

A woman from Berlin recalled how they stood in long lines to get an eight-day ration allowance in honor of Hitler's birthday. She said that no one could afford to miss rations of this type as food was so scarce. Rationing of food became severe from 1943.

German civilian ration card

British beach mine

## Beach defense

Mines were planted to defend possible invasion beaches in southern Britain and northern France.

# Lightning war

"Blitzkrieg" (German for "lightning war"), was a fast and ferocious military attack, used by Germany, where highly mobile Panzer (armored) forces blasted into enemy territory. When Poland was attacked, in September 1939, Britain and France declared war on Germany. From May to June 1940, Germany invaded France and the Low Countries, despite having fewer tanks and troops than the combined forces of Britain, France, and Belgium. But they did have air superiority, and triumphed by June 1940.

## Taking France

This photograph of Calais shows the devastation after a Blitzkrieg bombing raid. Such rapid destruction led to France's collapse within six weeks.

## Motorcycle advance

German Panzer units used motorcycles with sidecars to drive fast into enemy land ahead of the main army, surprising the enemy.

## War declared

*British newspaper announces the start of the war*

Britain and France declared war against Germany on September 3, 1939. But most European countries, including Switzerland and Spain, together with the US, remained neutral.

## Panzer attack

Tanks were the main power behind the Blitzkrieg (portrayed here in a film), supported by air bombers. They were so fast in crushing enemy positions they often had to wait for the infantry to catch up.

*Building stands among the rubble in aftermath of German bombing*

## Dive bombers

The Junkers Ju87 (Stuka) dive was the main attacking aircraft used during the Blitzkrieg. They were fitted with screaming sirens as they dived to drop their bombs.

*Dropping bomb*

**Stick grenade**

**Hand grenade**

## Throwing bombs

Grenades were used by the German infantry as they advanced into enemy territory, to kill enemy troops and clear buildings of snipers.

## Operation Weserübung

Nazi Germany invaded Denmark and Norway in April 1940 in an attack called Operation Weserübung. Though Norway had declared neutrality during the outbreak of the war, its occupation was a strategic necessity to Nazi Germany.

German convoy in Norway

## Storming Low Countries

In May 1940, heavily armed German troops poured into Belgium, Luxembourg, and the Netherlands. Their forces were no match for the German army and they soon surrendered.

# Occupation

People reacted differently to German occupation. Some joined the resistance or refused to cooperate; others supported the Germans' anticommunist and anti-Jewish policies. Most of them had no choice but to accept. France and Norway's governments collaborated with Germany. The leaders of Poland, Czechoslovakia, Norway, the Netherlands, Greece, Luxembourg, and Yugoslavia fled to London, where they set up governments in exile. The kings of Belgium and Denmark stayed, the former as a prisoner. The real power always lay with the occupying Germans.

Plaque of the LVF

## Brothers in arms

The French Légion des Volontaires Français (LVF) was anticommunist and raised volunteers to fight with the Germans against the USSR.

Homemade wireless receiver used by a Dutch family during the occupation

*Ear piece*

*Hitler visits Paris nine days after the Nazis took control*

## Hitler in Paris

German troops entered an undefended Paris on June 14, 1940. Two million citizens fled, but Parisian life continued much as before, with German officers mixing with locals. Hitler visited Paris nine days after the Nazis took control.

## Secret radio

Radios were forbidden in many occupied countries, so people made their own secret radios, such as this one used by a Dutch family to listen to the BBC. Broadcasts included war news, messages from exiled royals, and coded messages to secret agents.

*A French collaborator has her hair cropped*

## The collaborators

Throughout occupied Europe, many people collaborated with the Germans. As countries were liberated, some locals took revenge against the collaborators by beating or shooting them, or by shaving the women's heads.

## Operation Dynamo

Between May 26 and June 4, 1940, 338,226 soldiers were evacuated from the French beaches of Dunkirk. The German army sped through France toward the English Channel, trapping the British and French armies. Ships sailed back and forth to rescue the soldiers. The battle of France was a huge defeat for the British army as 90,000 troops were taken prisoner, but the successful evacuation raised morale.

*Lapel badge bearing the Vichy State double-headed ax*

## New symbols

During Vichy rule, many symbols of Republican France were replaced by Vichy symbols, such as the double-headed ax and portraits of Marshal Pétain.

*English Cross of St. George*

## Vichy France

On June 22, 1940, French leader Marshal Pétain agreed to German occupation in the north and west while he headed a puppet state, which was really controlled by Germany, from Vichy. His government collaborated with the Germans, but in November 1942, the Germans took over and the state collapsed in August 1944.

## To the rescue

At only 14 ft (4.4 m) long, *Tamzine* was the smallest of 900 boats in Operation Dynamo. Others ranged from minesweepers and destroyers to pleasure craft and fishing boats. *Tamzine* ferried many men from the beach to the deep-water vessels.

*Tamzine*, the smallest civilian vessel to cross the Channel during Operation Dynamo

# Resistance

## Showing support

Resistance groups often wore armbands like this one of the Polish Home Army, which led the Warsaw Uprising in August 1944 but was crushed.

## Helping hand

Dutch resistance groups, who sported the royal color orange, were very effective, providing support and shelter for Jews, and assisting Allied airborne troops.

## Free French forces

When France fell, General Charles de Gaulle fled to London and broadcast an appeal for people to fight for Free France.

## Danish spies

As conditions under the Germans worsened, a large Danish resistance spied for Britain and carried out strikes.

Armed resistance was initially scattered. Gradually, arms and intelligence from Britain supported organized groups, while Communist groups in Eastern Europe received help from the USSR after 1941. As the Germans became abusive toward peoples they deemed "subhuman," resistance increased. When liberation came (1944–1945), partisan groups were fighting with the British, US, and Soviet forces.

## King Christian X

When Germany invaded Denmark on April 9, 1940, King Christian X stayed. His government avoided cooperating with Germany and helped Jews escape.

## Freedom stamps

In June 1940, French General Charles de Gaulle set up the French Committee of National Liberation. This "Free French" government issued documents with official stamps such as these.

*Stamp on document for resistance medal*

Genuine stamp

Fake stamp

*Fake stamps show a larger bag under the left eye*

## Spot the difference

Communicating by mail was risky. The Germans intercepted letters from the French resistance, leading to the death of members. To make sure they knew which letters to trust, the British printed French stamps and changed one tiny detail.

## Brave widow

Violette Szabo joined the Special Operations Executive (SOE) after her husband died fighting for the Free French army. She was twice dropped into France, but was captured and died in a concentration camp.

## Attacking from the bushes

French resistance began as soon as the German armies entered France in May 1940. By 1941, there were a few organized, more effective, armed resistance groups (right), known as the Maquis (meaning bush or scrub) as they hid in the undergrowth, then sprung out to fight.

*Silencer eliminates most of the sound of the blast*

*Skeleton butt—a lightweight frame*

*Trigger*

## Silent weapons

This silenced 9-mm Beretta pistol was used by the Organizzazione per la Vigilanza e la Repressione dell'Antifascismov (OVRA), set up to suppress resistance to Italian Fascism.

## Danish guns

This 9-mm Mark II submachine gun was built by the Danish resistance, based on the British Sten, which was light, simple to use, and easy and cheap to make.

## Tito's Partisans

The most successful European resistance group, the Yugoslav Partisans, was organized by Communist Party leader Tito with 150,000 members. In 1944, combined Partisan and Soviet Red Army forces regained Yugoslavia from the Germans.

# German army

The German armed services were a tangle of different organizations, each reporting to Hitler as Commander-in-Chief, including the Wehrmacht (the main army); the Schutzstaffel (SS)—originally Hitler's bodyguard with many secret police (Gestapo) in the ranks; the armed Panzer (tank) divisions; the navy (Kriegsmarine); the air force (Luftwaffe); the reserve forces; the militias; and the Brownshirts. Uniforms and emblems gave a strong identity and attracted a young, loyal force.

## Heavy armor

Tank troops belonged to the Panzer (German for armor) army. The PzKpfw IV (right) was one of 2,500 tanks that rolled into France in 1940.

*Army officer with eagle insignia on his breast pocket*

## The Nazi eagle

This national emblem badge was worn by the Waffen-SS—the combat divisions of the SS. At its peak in 1942–1943, it had 39 divisions with more than 900,000 soldiers.

*Eagle*

*Swastika—an ancient symbol for good luck.*

*National emblem*

## The Wehrmacht

Although the Wehrmacht offcially comprised all units of the German military, it was commonly used to refer to the land army—the Heer. By the end of World War II, about 13 million troops had served in the land army. This illustration shows Wehrmacht soldiers on the battlefield in 1942.

*Loops to tow gun*

## Hidden horrors

The Germans' antitank Pak 38 (left) was the only gun able to tackle the well-armored Soviet T34 tanks. It had a range of 9,022 ft (2,750 m) and its low silhouette could be hidden.

*Solid, low-maintenance wheels*

## Luftwaffe

The German air force, shown on this poster, was the most advanced and experienced air force in the world during the outbreak of World War II.

## SS Panzer uniform

SS Panzer troops wore a black, tight, short jacket (*panzerjacke*), suited for inside the cramped tanks. Their field cap bore the national emblem and the SS death's head.

Field cap

SS Panzer jacket

Belt

SS motto "Meine Ehre heisst Treue" (Loyalty is my honor)

Oak and laurel leaves

Rank badge for Major General

General officer's cap

Field service tunic

Division "Grossdeutschland" (Greater Germany)

Belt with holster

General officer's breeches

Broad red stripes indicate the wearer was an army general

Ankle slit

Edging

Trousers

Boots

## SS officer uniform

Hitler's new national emblem—a swastika clutched by an eagle—was added to all army uniforms. He kept much traditional army insignia, such as badges for rank. Colored piping showed army branches, such as white for infantry.

## On the battle line

More than 12.5 million infantry (foot soldiers, like the man here) played a major role in the German army, fighting all the way to the outskirts of Moscow before retreating to defend Berlin.

Six barrels were fired consecutively, one second apart

## Moaning Minnie

The nebelwerfer (fog thrower, nicknamed "Moaning Minnie" due to the noise it made) fired 70-lb (32-kg) rockets up to 22,639 ft (6,900 m), but each rocket gave itself away with a 40-ft (12-m) bright flame.

# The Battle of Britain

With the fall of France in June 1940, Hitler hoped Britain might settle for peace. But Britain's new leader Winston Churchill had no such intention. So Hitler planned to launch a seaborne invasion—Operation Sea Lion. For this to work, the German air force (Luftwaffe) had to defeat the British Royal Air Force (RAF). From July to October 1940, battles raged across the sky above southeast England and the RAF slowly won control.

## Spitfire

The RAF's Spitfire Mk 1A could fly at speeds up to 362 mph (582 kph). It was faster at high altitudes and more maneuverable than the German Messerschmitt Bf109E.

*Eight Browning machine guns in edges of wings*

*Two RAF navigators (left) study a map with their Polish pilots*

## International air force

The RAF had pilots from all around the world who had fled their German-occupied countries. New pilots received a maximum of only ten hours training before being sent up to fight.

*Mobile antiaircraft radar receiver*

## Detection

RAF radar systems used 300-ft (90-m) steel masts to emit radio signals. The signals bounced off enemy planes and were picked up by radar receivers, alerting pilots to resume battle in the air. This new technology helped Britain win the war.

## Dogfights

As the RAF and the Luftwaffe fought for control of the skies, dogfights (close-up battles between fighter aircraft) were common, as portrayed here in the film *Battle of Britain*.

*Heinkel He 111 bomber in dogfight during Battle of Britain*

*Fighter plane shot down during dogfight*

*Twin fins on tail*

## Messerschmitts

Two types of Messerschmitts formed the fighter mainstay of the Luftwaffe. The Bf110C, an escort fighter for long-range bombers, was slow, hard to handle, and inferior to the British Hurricanes and Spitfires. The Bf109E was faster, but its 410-mile (660-km) range limited its effect.

### 👁 EYEWITNESS

**Tom Neil (1920–2018)**
A British aviator and a flying ace in the RAF, Neil shot down 14 enemy aircraft and flew 141 combat missions during the Battle of Britain. He said, "The dread of being burned to death was one of the worst fears."

## On watch

Ground crews used powerful and sturdy binoculars, such as these used by the Luftwaffe, to watch for enemy aircraft. Both sides used radar for long-distance observations. In the air, combat pilots had to stay alert for enemy aircraft.

*Direction finder*

*Eyepiece*

*Binoculars rotate for an all-around view of the skies*

## Göring's air force

Luftwaffe Chief, Reichsmarschall Hermann Göring, watched the Battle of Britain from the French coast. He believed they could destroy air defenses in southern England in four days and the RAF in four weeks. But the Luftwaffe failed.

# Bombing raids

## Bombers

With bomb loads up to 4,000 lb (1,825 kg), heavy bombers like these US Flying Fortresses could do immense damage.

The terrifying drone of enemy bomber planes heralded mass destruction. Each side believed that bombing strategic targets, such as factories, railroads, and oil refineries, would cripple the enemy war effort and destroy their morale. Thus, Britain endured the Blitz from 1940–1941, while Germany was bombed repeatedly from 1942 and Japan from 1944.

## Fire fighting

Most bomb damage was caused by the fires they ignited. Firefighters risked their lives to keep the flames under control, and to save anyone trapped in the burning buildings.

## Air-raid survival

During air raids, people hid in underground shelters, in cellars, or in makeshift shelters in their own homes. Despite heavy bombing of cities, many people survived.

British fire service badge

NFS

*Air-raid wardens and civilians search for survivors among the wreckage*

## The Blitz

Germany tried to force Britain to surrender during September 1940 to May 1941 by bombing its major cities, including London, Liverpool, Glasgow, and Belfast. More than 60,000 civilians were killed and two million homes destroyed in "the Blitz."

# Bombing of Dresden

The Allied bombing of the German city of Dresden in February 1945 created a firestorm, destroying the city and killing 30,000–60,000 civilians. With few military targets, many condemned the raid as a war crime.

*Dresden still in ruins two years after the raid*

👁 **EYEWITNESS**

### Dambusters raid

In 1943, a bomber raid by Royal Air Force No. 617 Squadron destroyed important German dams. Originally named Operation Chastise, it is also known as the Dambusters raid. Guy Gibson (right) was the pilot leader of the Dambusters.

*Gun sight*

**Rear machine gun from a Heinkel bomber**

## Bomber machine gun

Gunners with powerful machine guns were the slow-flying, heavily laden bombers' only defense. When possible, the bombers flew in large convoys escorted by fast, nimble fighter planes to fend off any attack.

## Defend the pilot

Gunners on bomber planes sat or stood in exposed gun turrets to give them a clear view of the skies and any enemy aircraft.

## German gunner award

The Luftwaffe awarded its war service badge to gunners on a points system; shooting down one enemy aircraft was 4 points; 16 points achieved the award.

*V-2 was 46 ft (14 m) long, weighed 28,660 lb (13,000 kg), and flew at an altitude of 50 miles (80 km)*

**Magnesium incendiary bomb**

## Incendiary bombs

Thousands of these bombs were dropped on British and German cities; combustible chemicals created immense heat to set buildings alight.

## Bomb power

Late in the war, Germany launched its most secret and deadly weapons. They were the V-1 flying bomb and the V-2 rocket (V stood for vengeance). Both bombs carried warheads that weighed around one ton. They were capable of great damage.

**V-2 rocket**

# Total war

Until mid-1941, the war was mainly in Europe and North Africa, between the Axis (Germany, Italy, and some east European countries) and the Allies (Britain, France, and their empires). After France fell, Britain stood alone, but then Germany invaded the USSR, and Japan attacked the US at Pearl Harbor and the British in Malaya. The war was then fought worldwide.

## OCCUPIED EUROPE

By 1942, Germany and Italy occupied most of Europe. The Allies occupied Morocco and Algeria, and drove the Germans from Egypt to Libya.

- Axis states
- Areas controlled by Axis
- Allied states
- Areas controlled by Allies
- Neutral states
- -- Extent of German military occupation

**Map showing the extent of Axis control in Europe in 1942**

*USS Arizona sinks after Japanese bombs hit its ammunition magazine*

## Into USSR

On June 22, 1941, the Germans attacked the Soviets in Operation Barbarossa. This broke the 1939 Nazi-Soviet Pact and brought the USSR into the war on the same side as Britain. Seen below are German Panzer units passing through a blazing Russian village, torched by fleeing civilians.

*British Prime Minister Winston Churchill (1874-1965)*

*US President Franklin Roosevelt (1882-1945)*

*Soviet leader Josef Stalin (1878-1953)*

### The big three

The leaders of Britain, the USSR, and the US met twice during the war (seen here in February 1945) to coordinate their war efforts.

> "Yesterday, December 7, 1941—
> **a date that will live in infamy**—the United States of America was suddenly and deliberately attacked by naval and air forces of the Empire of Japan ..."
> —Franklin D. Roosevelt (1941)

USS *Arizona* under attack

## Pearl Harbor attack

On December 7, 1941, Japan attacked the US naval base of Pearl Harbor in Hawaii destroying 19 ships and killing 2,403 sailors. On December 8, Congress declared war on Japan and Germany.

## Fighting for France

When Germany invaded France, General Charles de Gaulle (right) went to Britain and raised the banner of Free France, leading overseas French troops and resistance fighters.

## Mussolini's Italy

Mussolini (right) and Italy did not join Germany's side until June 1940, when it declared war on Britain and France. Italian troops fought with the Germans in the USSR, but Italy always remained the junior partner in the Axis.

Hitler and Mussolini drive through Florence, Italy

## General Hideki Tojo

Tojo led Japan's pro-military party and became prime minister in October 1941. He sided with Germany and Italy, had Japan attack US and British territory in Asia, and extended Japan's empire. He was tried for war crimes in 1948 and executed.

General Hideki Tojo on the cover of a magazine

### JAPANESE CONTROL

By 1942, Japan controlled southeast Asia and much of the Pacific. In June 1942, the US halted the Japanese advance at Midway.

- ⬜ Japanese-controlled area by 1942
- ┅ Extent of Japanese expansion

Map showing the extent of Japanese control in 1942

# In enemy territory

Many individuals risked their lives by entering enemy-occupied countries to spy, work with resistance fighters, and sabotage enemy plans. The British set up the Special Operations Executive (SOE) and the Americans formed the Office of Strategic Services (OSS), to train spies and devise ways to hide equipment for a mission. Many spies were killed, or captured, tortured, and sent to concentration camps.

## Suicide pill
British spies carried a lethal pill (L-pill), to be swallowed if they were captured by the enemy. The pill killed in five seconds. Agents concealed the pills in lockets, rings, and other jewelry.

## Secret agent Sorge
Richard Sorge, as seen on this Soviet stamp, was a German journalist spying for the USSR. He learned that Japan was to attack Asia, not the USSR, in 1941, which freed up Soviet troops to fight Germany.

Barrel — — Tobacco bowl

## Pipe pistol
This pipe pistol was designed to look like a smoking pipe for use by Special Operations Executive (SOE) personnel. Bullets would be fired by removing the mouthpiece and twisting the tobacco bowl.

Blade — Holes cut for display

## Hidden knife
MI9, a British organization that helped prisoners of war escape, designed this pencil to hide a blade, so as not to arouse suspicion during a search.

End unscrewed to load

Cartridge

## Propelling pencil pistol
By inserting a 6.35-mm cartridge, this pencil became a pistol. The casing contained a spring-loaded hammer to fire the cartridge, released by a button on the side.

Button pulled back to fire

## Poison pen threat
Made by the British, this pen fired a gramophone needle when the cap was pulled back and released. It was not lethal—the idea was that users would spread a rumor that the needles were poisoned.

Tuning dial

Cover with English labels

## Pocket radio
Abwehr (German military intelligence) issued agents with this small radio to transmit Morse code. All labels were in English so as not to betray its user.

Straps fastened the rubber sole over agent's boots

## Footprint disguise
The SOE's feet-shaped rubber soles attached to boots for use on a beach to fool the Japanese into thinking they were locals' footprints.

### 👁 EYEWITNESS

**Dangerous date**
The SOE sent Odette Sansom to link up with a French Resistance unit, led by Peter Churchill. Both were captured, but they survived and married after the war.

## Secrets underfoot

Compartments inside boots' rubber heels made ideal hiding places for papers. Both sides used this during the war, but it was often the first place searched when captured.

*Message hidden in the heel*

## Messages from a suitcase

Suitcase radios were used by both sides to broadcast messages from inside enemy territory. Messages were transmitted in Morse code, using a system of sounds in place of letters.

*Headphones allowed agents to listen to incoming messages*

*Plug connected transmitter to electricity*

## Fighter and spy

A French Resistance fighter and a British spy, Nancy Wake saved hundreds of Allied soldiers during the war. She joined the SOE and in 1944 parachuted into France, where she collected parachute drops of weapons to help Allied forces.

## Card tricks

An escape map, divided into numbered sections, was hidden inside playing cards. Escapees would soak the tops and reorder the sections to plot their route home.

*Top of card peeled off to reveal map*

## A foreign match

This matchbox looks French but was made in Britain for SOE agents. Spies abroad could not take anything that might betray their true identity.

*Frequency dial*

*Spare valve*

*Lens opening*

## Matchbox camera

Britain and the United States developed this camera so OSS agents could take pictures secretly. The front label was changed according to the country they were in.

*Key used to tap out Morse code*

This Mark II radio was used by Oluf Reed Olsen, a Norwegian agent working for Britain

*Crystal plug used to change transmission frequency*

*Battery clips connected transmitter to car battery for use without utility power*

# The prisoners

Millions of soldiers were captured or surrendered to enemy forces. Most of these prisoners of war (POWs) spent months or years locked up in specially built prisons. The Geneva Convention of 1929 stated that prisoners were to be treated well. Many attempted to escape, but few succeeded. Civilians were detained at internment camps, including the Germans in the United Kingdom and the Japanese in the United States.

## Camp currency
Allied POWs in German camps were paid with special camp money (*Lagergeld*) for their work. These Reichsmark notes, could buy toothpaste, soap, and sometimes extra food rations.

## Happy to be alive
In April 1945, 9,000 Soviet POWs were freed by the US from the German Stalag 326 camp. Soviet POWs were treated appallingly by the Germans, made to walk for weeks to camps and given starvation rations.

## Life in captivity
The Geneva Convention stated that POWs must be clothed, given food and lodgings as good as their guards, allowed to keep possessions, practice their religion, and receive medical treatment. It was not always kept.

## Marked men
All POWs had to carry identification (ID) tags with them at all times. These two came from the Oflag XVIIA and Stalag VI/A camps in Germany.

Homemade plane and saw

## Men with a mission
The tools, made from bedposts and scraps of metal, were used in Colditz to build the escape glider.

## Flying away
The building of this glider in Colditz Castle, Germany, was one of many escape plans from this high-security camp. Of the 1,500 POWs there, 176 attempted to escape, but only 31 succeeded.

Food parcels contained luxuries not available in camp

## A rare treat

Under the Geneva Convention, POWs could receive letters and gifts from home. These were organized by the International Red Cross in Geneva, Switzerland. They kept prisoners in touch with their families and gave them treats to eat.

## Buckle blade

Some prisoners snuck in tools. A blade hidden on a belt could help cut them free if they were tied up.

*Miniature saw blade*

## Clever gadgets

Punch daggers, maps, or messages were hidden inside the hollow handles of safety razors and false bottoms of shaving brushes. POWs were allowed to keep such items that were part of mess kits.

## Button compass

A tiny compass could be hidden in a button for navigating to safety.

*Compass needle*

Flying boot

## Escape boot

British RAF pilots wore boots that could be cut into civilian shoes with a hidden penknife so they could blend into enemy territory and avoid capture.

👁 **EYEWITNESS**

### Living with the enemy

After the war, not all prisoners were returned home immediately, but they could befriend the locals. Ludwig Maier (second right), a German architect imprisoned in Scotland, wed English woman Lucy Tupper in 1947.

## Camp crocodiles

POWs, like these Germans, often traveled hundreds of miles to reach a camp. Italians captured in North Africa were taken to Australia, South Africa, and India; 50,000 other Italians went to the US.

# Code-breakers

A code replaces words with letters or symbols. A cipher is a form of code that adds or substitutes letters to disguise it. Both sides used codes and ciphers for messages during the war. Some Allied cryptographers (code-breakers) cracked the Axis codes, revealing valuable information that gave the Allies considerable advantage over their enemies.

*Spare light bulbs*

*Viewing windows on lid show encoded letters*

*Position of rotors controls encoding of each letter; rotors spin after each letter*

*Rotor cylinder carries three (later four) alphabetical rotors*

*Alphabetical light board shows final encoded letter*

*Keyboard to type in message*

*Plugboard settings are changed daily*

*Light filter plate*

Klappe schließen

## Early computers

Scientists and cryptographers at Bletchley Park (the British code-breaking center) developed the "bombe" to decipher German Enigma messages. As Enigma grew more complex, they built Colossus, a forerunner of modern electronic computers.

### 👁 EYEWITNESS

**Alan Turing**
Mathematician Alan Turing was one of the brilliant code-breakers working for British Intelligence during the war. He played a key role in deciphering the German Enigma.

## The German Enigma cipher

The Enigma was a German cipher machine in use during World War II. It enciphered each letter with alphabetical rotors, placed on a cylinder in a predetermined order, and a set of plugs in a plugboard. The settings varied each day, giving trillions of possible combinations. Other countries had their own cipher machines.

## An inside ring

Everyday objects were used to hide microdots—tiny photographs of a coded message that can be read only with a magnifying viewer.

*Secret chamber*

*Screw top*

**Boris Hagelin**

## The converted

In the 1930s, Swedish cryptographer, Boris Hagelin invented the Converter M-209. It was the main cipher machine used by the US Army during the war.

## Fact to fiction

Some code-breakers and spies turned their experiences into fiction, such as Ian Fleming, who worked for British Naval Intelligence.

*Ian Fleming, creator of the fictional spy James Bond*

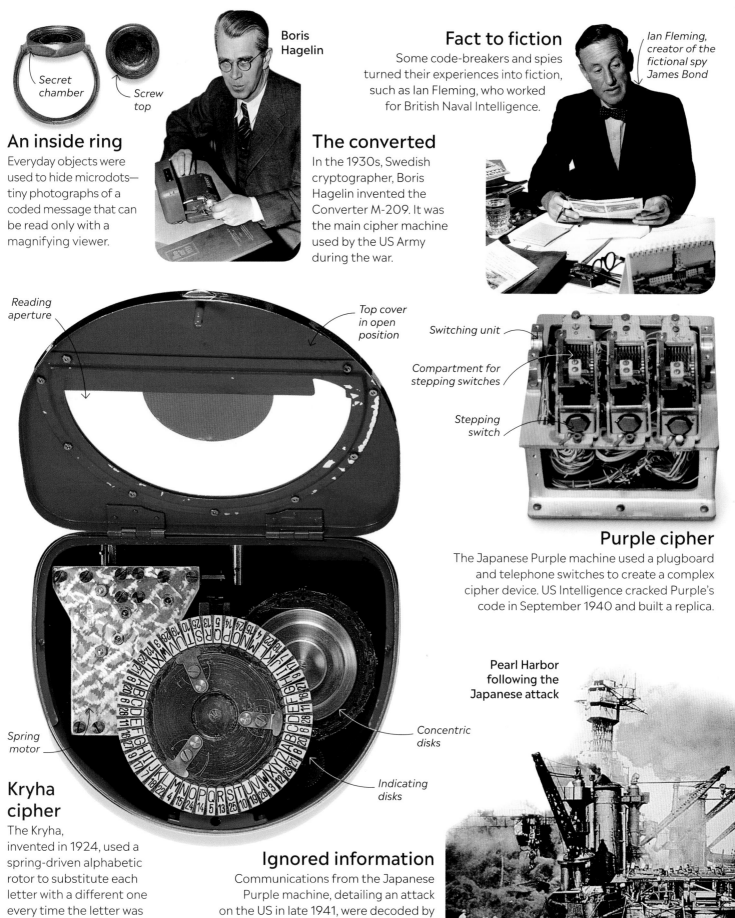

*Reading aperture*

*Top cover in open position*

*Switching unit*

*Compartment for stepping switches*

*Stepping switch*

## Purple cipher

The Japanese Purple machine used a plugboard and telephone switches to create a complex cipher device. US Intelligence cracked Purple's code in September 1940 and built a replica.

*Spring motor*

*Concentric disks*

*Indicating disks*

**Pearl Harbor following the Japanese attack**

## Kryha cipher

The Kryha, invented in 1924, used a spring-driven alphabetic rotor to substitute each letter with a different one every time the letter was used in a word. The Germans used the Kryha in the war, not realizing that the US had already broken its code.

## Ignored information

Communications from the Japanese Purple machine, detailing an attack on the US in late 1941, were decoded by the US, but the Pearl Harbor target was not clear until it was too late. Code-breaking in 1942 enabled the US to defeat the Japanese navy at Midway.

Pocket-size novel for US troops

# America at war

After the shock of Pearl Harbor, the US transformed its economy into a giant war machine, mass-producing every weapon to win on land, sea, and air. Expenditure on war production rose massively, unemployment disappeared, and wages doubled. Unlike every other country at war, the US boomed and most people had more money to spend than ever before.

## Mass production

Aircraft factories played a major role in turning out arms. In total, US factories built 250,000 aircraft, 90,000 tanks, 350 destroyer ships, and 200 submarines. By 1944, they produced 40 percent of world arms.

## Browning machine gun

The 0.5 Browning machine gun was the standard weapon in US bombers. But even flying in close formation with others, the Browning was no match for German fighter planes.

*Spring-loaded pilot parachute*

*Four main parachutes for a gentle descent*

*Steel parachute cable*

### 15th Air Force

*Crashpan to cushion wheels on landing*

### 9th Air Force

## Fighting with fire

Flamethrowers (such as used by this US marine on Guadalcanal in the Pacific, 1942) were often used to set fire to buildings or destroy protective vegetation, to flush out the enemy.

US Strategic Air Forces

## US Army Air Force (USAAF) badges

The 15th Air Force in southern Italy bombed German-held targets. The 9th supported the Allies in North Africa and Italy. The 8th, 9th, and 15th later merged into the US Strategic Air Forces in Europe.

Maximum speed
was 437 mph
(703 kph)

The Mustang's
range was
2,080 miles
(3,347 km)

Droppable
fuel tank

# Long-range fighter

Early versions of the NAA P-51D Mustang were limited in altitude and range, but a better engine, larger fuel tanks, and a cut-down rear fuselage made the fourth version (P-51 D) one of the best fighter planes of the war. It was used to defend bombers over Germany.

👁 **EYEWITNESS**

**Navajo code talkers**
Native American Navajo, fluent in their own language and English, were used by the US marines, to transmit secret Allied messages in the Pacific War.

## B-24 liberator

Having flown all the way from southern Italy, this B-24 Liberator (a heavy bomber with a long range) is flying low as it bombs oil fields in southern Romania.

North American Aviation (NAA) P-51 D Mustang

Central support to which parachutes are attached

Bag for empty cartridge cases

Machine gun

## Parachute jeep

US Army jeeps could be dropped by parachute. Developed in 1940, the US jeep was one of the best loved (and envied) of all war vehicles. Its four-wheel drive made it versatile in most terrains.

Protective headgear used in turrets and other combat positions where standard helmets were too big

**US aircrew M4 helmet**

US jeep could carry an 800-lb (360-kg) load and tow an antitank gun at the same time

Flak jacket weighed 20 lb (9 kg)

Supporting cradle

Parachute release stand

## Taking the flak

Flak jackets such as this were worn by US aircrew from 1942 to protect them from antiaircraft fire. By 1944, 13,500 were used by the 8th Air Force in Europe.

# Women **at work**

### New recruits

As more men were required for fighting, posters promising glamour attracted more women into the war effort.

Before World War II, most women worked within the home. However, with men away fighting, almost every task that had previously been restricted to men was now taken over by women. Women also played an important role in resistance forces. The war could not have been waged and won without women's vital contribution. After the war, attitudes toward women in the workplace changed forever.

*A woman assists with aircraft maintenance*

**Henry Arnold, commanding general of the US Army Air Forces**

**"Now in 1944, it is on record that women can fly as well as men."**

### Night watch

Many women operated the powerful searchlights that tracked enemy bombers for antiaircraft guns to fire at before the bombers dropped their bombs. Women were not allowed to actually fire the guns, though. Night work could also mean patrolling the streets as an air-raid warden.

*Female searchlight operator scours the night sky for bombers*

### Air-raid training

In India, fear of a Japanese invasion led the government to take precautionary steps, training women for air-raid precaution (ARP) duties and as auxiliaries to support troops in the Far East.

## Nazi mothers

In Germany, mothers were awarded medals for producing target numbers of children. The Nazis idealized German women as mothers of the new "master race."

Silver (2nd class) medal awarded for bearing six to seven children

Gas mask chamber

## Gas bag

Everyone had to keep their gas masks with them. This handbag has a special compartment for a mask, although most people carried theirs in cardboard boxes, which women often decorated with fabric.

## Land girls

One of women's major contributions to the war effort was to run the farms and grow much-needed food. In Britain, the Women's Land Army recruited 77,000 members to carry out arduous tasks, such as plowing and harvesting.

## Aircraft maintenance

The shortage of male pilots and mechanics meant that many women learned to fly and maintain planes, delivering and servicing them. Seen on the left is a woman assisting with aircraft maintenance.

## Pans to planes

Due to the scarcity of iron, tin, and aluminum, posters appealed to housewives for unwanted items. Old pots and pans were melted down for planes. Even old woolen clothes were unraveled and knitted into socks and scarves for the troops.

*Frying pan made from the wreckage of a German plane*

## Rosie the Riveter

In the US, fictional character Rosie the Riveter became a symbol of the new working woman, as women were needed in factories to replace the 16 million US citizens called into the armed services.

GOOD BYE
ANSPORT

## Growing up in Japan

In school, Japanese children were told their country was superior and their duty was to fight for their emperor. They had to attend military drills and work in the student labor force. When Japanese cities were bombed by the US, 450,000 children were evacuated out of the cities.

— Protective eyepiece

— Air filter

"Mickey Mouse" gas mask

## Novelty

Colorful "Mickey Mouse" gas masks were issued to British toddlers to make them more fun. Children were taught how to put their masks on in a hurry.

# A wartime childhood

Children were as affected by the war as the adults. Their homes were bombed or burned, their fathers were called up to fight, and their mothers went to work. For one group of children in particular the war brought special fear, as the German authorities sought out Jewish children and sent them to die in concentration camps. For all children, the war robbed them of an education and a normal life.

## Evacuees

The war separated many youngsters from their families. During the Blitz, thousands of British children went to live with foster families in the countryside, or even overseas. All evacuees wore labels indicating their destination. Evacuees were allowed to take one toy.

## Forced to follow Hitler

At first, membership of the Hitler Youth was voluntary. But in 1936, it was made compulsory for all children aged 10 to 18.

## Blitz games

Many themed toys and games, such as this evacuation card game, were produced in the war years. Card games were popular for the long hours spent in air-raid shelters.

## Nazi toys

Propaganda infected all aspects of German life. Even toys glorified the "Aryan" (blond-haired, blue-eyed) race as masters of the world, and put down the Jews.

## 👁 EYEWITNESS

### In hiding

For two years, Jewish girl Anne Frank and her family hid from the Nazis in an attic in the Netherlands, where Anne kept a diary. But the family was betrayed and Anne died of typhus in Belsen concentration camp in March 1945.

## For Motherland

As the German army swept into the USSR in 1941, many children became orphaned and homeless. Some joined the partisan groups fighting the Germans, running messages, fetching supplies, and even taking part in acts of sabotage.

## Young Nazis

In 1926, the Hitler Youth became the male youth division of the Nazi Party (girls joined the League of German Girls). In 1943, those aged 16 were called up to fight. Younger recruits helped on farms or delivered mail.

# The Pacific

After their surprise attack on Pearl Harbor in December 1941, the Japanese swarmed all over southeast Asia and advanced, island by island, across the Pacific, south toward Australia and east to the US. Their aim was to form a huge empire with supplies of all raw materials needed to build military power. Japan seemed invincible, but two massive naval battles—in the Coral Sea in May 1942 and at Midway in June 1942—halted their advance.

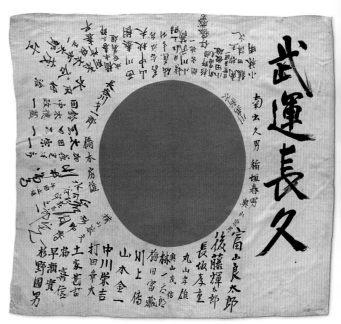

## Japanese prayer flag

Japanese servicemen carried, or wore around their heads, prayer flags into battle, with prayers and blessings written by relatives on the background of the flag of Japan.

## Aircraft carrier

Douglas Devastator torpedo bombers (left) were old and lumbering planes used by the US on aircraft carriers. They proved no match for the speedy Japanese Mitsubishi A6M Zero fighters, which knocked out all but four of the USS *Enterprise*'s bombers. But overall, the Japanese suffered a defeat at Midway.

*Douglas Devastator bombers prepare for action*

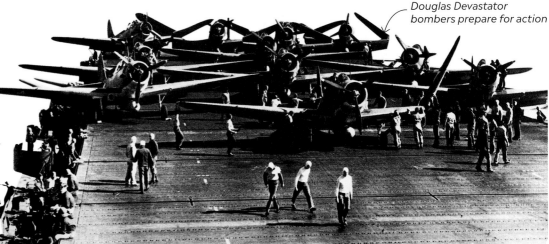

## The Coral Sea

The Japanese tried to capture island bases to use for air attacks on Australia. But the US halted their advance south in May 1942 in the first naval battle conducted entirely by aircraft taking off from carriers.

*A Japanese aircraft floats in tatters in the Coral Sea after being shot down*

# Suicide missions

The battle for the Philippines raged in October 1944, and the desperate Japanese introduced a terrifying weapon: volunteer bomber pilots (Kamikazes) flew planes loaded with explosives onto the decks of US warships to blow them up.

## Struggle for Guadalcanal Island

US aircraft carrier *Hornet* is under fire from Japanese aircraft at the Battle of Santa Cruz in October 1942. This sea battle was one of many fought around Guadalcanal as Japanese and US forces fought for this strategic base. The US took over the island in February 1943, but Japan's ferocious resistance showed how far they would go to defend territory.

*A Malayan currency note issued during Japanese invasion*

## Invasion of Malaya

The Japanese invasion of Malaya (now a part of Malaysia) lasted from December 1941 to January 1942. Malaya was rich in natural resources such as tin and rubber, and provided a barrier around Japanese conquests.

*Scale showing degrees north or south of equator*

## Japanese sextants

The Japanese Navy used sextants to navigate the vast Pacific. Its navy was the third largest in the world (after the US and Britain) with 10 aircraft carriers, 12 battleships, 38 cruisers, 124 destroyers, and a mighty naval air force.

*Adjustable eyepiece*

**Japanese naval sextant for calculating latitude (distance north or south)**

*Horizon mirror*

*Kamikaze pilot ties a hachimaki around his head*

## Masked

Japanese pilots wore protective leather masks, which made them look as fierce as their reputation. Most would kill themselves before surrendering.

## Kamikaze pilot

Japanese pilots volunteered for the Kamikaze, certain-death, flights believing it glorious to die for their emperor, or inspired by Japanese military traditions of self-sacrifice. They wore the *hachimaki* (headcloth) of the medieval samurai.

# Japan

Naval and military ensign

Throughout the war, the Japanese fought on three fronts: for occupation of China in the north; in an island-hopping campaign against the US, Australian, and New Zealand forces in the Pacific Ocean; and in the jungles of Burma, where the "forgotten war" continued against the British and Indian armies and the Chindits (a British-Burmese fighting unit) who fought to liberate Burma. Many Japanese fought to the death.

Australian "Austen" submachine gun

## Australia

Australian forces were heavily involved in the war against Japan—preventing the Japanese from occupying Papua New Guinea in 1942, and liberating New Guinea and other islands with the US—as Japan's expansion in southeast Asia threatened Australia.

## Portable communications

Field telephones were used by Allied and Japanese soldiers. The speed of the Japanese advances meant troops needed to inform headquarters of their progress and on the whereabouts of the enemy.

## Loyal fighters

More than 1,700,000 Japanese soldiers obeyed the Soldier Code of 1942, based on the ancient Bushido (warrior) Code of the samurai fighters, which stated soldiers must be loyal to the emperor and be willing to die in combat rather than face the shame of capture.

*A Japanese soldier holds the Rising Sun flag*

### Saved from starvation

These Dutch POWs were lucky; a quarter of the 103,000 Australian, US, British, and Dutch soldiers taken captive by the Japanese had died in camps by 1944. Asian prisoners suffered worse— at least 100,000 died building the Thailand-Burma railroad alone.

## Thailand–Burma railroad

The Japanese used diesel-powered traction cars, that could run on rails or roads from 1942–1943. With them, they built a railroad from Thailand to Burma, intending to use it to quickly move troops and supplies through their empire.

## Liberating Burma

The battle for Burma was fought on the road between the Indian cities of Kohima and Imphal. The British used Imphal as their base after the Japanese expelled them from Burma in May 1942. The Japanese invaded India in March 1944. British and Indian troops (left) defeated a force of 80,000 and paved the way for Burma's liberation (achieved May 1945).

## Bridge attack

Railroad bridges along the 258-mile (415-km) long Thailand-Burma railroad were designed and built by POWs. British planes regularly bombed the bridges, hoping to destroy the railroad and halt the Japanese.

## Raising the flag

In February 1945, US marines stormed Iwo Jima, a tiny island south of Japan. The Japanese defended the island to the bitter end. After suffering losses, the US bombed mainland Japanese cities and later dropped two atomic bombs.

Improvised glasses and comb

A US memorial of marines hoisting the flag on Mt. Suribachi, Iwo Jima

## Captured

POWs held by the Japanese were given few provisions and had to improvise. The Japanese had no respect for POWs, and worked many of them to death building railroads and roads.

41

# The battle of the Atlantic

Throughout the war, a battle raged in the North Atlantic Ocean between the Allies and the Germans, as German U-boats (submarines) and destroyers attacked supply ships from the US. The German navy was smaller than the Allies', but its U-boats reigned supreme. However, the Allies' greater use of the convoy system, long-range aircraft patrols, quick-response antisubmarine warships, and improved radar saw the battle turn in the Allies' favor by mid-1943.

### Dig for victory

Overseas imports of food were hampered by the war. In Britain, to ensure supplies of fruit and vegetables, a "Dig for Victory" campaign urged people to grow food. Every spare bit of fertile land became vegetable patches.

... every available piece of land must be cultivated

GROW YOUR OWN FOOD
supply your own cookhouse

Equipped with 88 guns including 20 long-range and 68 antiaircraft guns

### Sinking the *Bismarck*

One of the largest—and allegedly unsinkable—German battleships, the *Bismarck*, set off from Gdynia in the Baltic on May 18, 1941, sailed around Iceland, sank Britain's HMS *Hood*, and was then destroyed by a British fleet on May 27.

Periscope

Wet-and-dry exit and reentry chamber

Main steering wheel

Helmsman's seat

Distilled water tank

Log tank

First lieutenant's seat frame

Wooden deckboard

Freshwater tank

### Inside a midget

The British X-craft midget submarine, crewed by four, handled special missions during the Battle of the Atlantic. One submarine disabled the German battleship *Tirpitz*, which threatened British convoys heading to the USSR.

### German Biber

Armed with two torpedoes, Biber submarines operated off the coast of northern France and the Netherlands from 1944–1945, damaging Allied cargo and cross-Channel ships supplying forces in western Europe.

Periscope

Viewing port

Towing eye

Warhead

Lieutenant Burkard Von Müllenheim-Rechberg, *Bismarck* survivor

# "We all ... glanced at the flag, and jumped ...
**In the water we were pushed together in a bunch, as we bobbed up and down like corks."**

## Up periscope

Safe beneath the surface, U-boat crews used periscopes to watch Allied convoys and select targets for their torpedoes and guns. But when U-boats were close to the surface, they were easily detectable from the air and Allied planes destroyed many of them.

*U-boat officer uses a periscope to locate enemy ships*

*The ship was 823 ft (251 m) long*

*Gun is aimed ready to fire at enemy ships and U-boats*

## Under attack

When under water, U-boats were vulnerable to depth charges dropped from Allied ships or aircraft; on the surface, to bombs, torpedoes, or shells; and in shallow waters, to mines. Only a quarter of German submarines survived the war.

*A sailor on board a warship accompanying an Atlantic convoy keeps a lookout for enemy aircraft*

## Atlantic convoy

Single merchant ships crossing the North Atlantic were vulnerable to attack from U-boats and so traveled in large convoys with warships and air cover. Convoys traveled at the speed of their slowest member, making it very dangerous, and many sailors died.

*Torpedo*

*Rudder*

*Propeller*

# Stalingrad

German bronze tank assault badge

Germany invaded the Soviet Union in 1941. The German army advanced north toward Leningrad, nearly reached Moscow in the east but was defeated by the weather, and then south to the wheat fields, oil wells, and Stalingrad—important because it was named after the Soviet leader, Stalin. The battle for Stalingrad saw vast losses on both sides. In early 1943, the eventual defeat of the German army and its surrender marked a turning point in the war—they were no longer unbeatable.

## In the snow

War in the Soviet Union was aggravated by the freezing Soviet winter, for which the Germans were ill-equipped. The Soviets were more used to it and had quilted undersuits, white camouflaged oversuits, fur hats, and felt boots.

## Red Army weaponry

Thousands of submachine guns, such as this PPS43, were cheaply and quickly made and issued to the Red Army.

*Trigger*

*Hooded foresight*

*Forward hand grip*

*Hand grip*

Soviet submachine gun

*Shoulder butt*

## Hand grenades

Soviets used these to stop the enemy advance in Stalingrad.

## Standard issue

The 7.62-mm Tokarev TT33 semiautomatic pistol was the standard issue gun given to Soviet officers, airmen, and tank crews.

## Battle of Stalingrad

In August 1942, the German 6th Army attacked from the west and pushed the defenders into buildings along the Volga River. The Soviets counterattacked in November, encircling the 6th Army. The Germans were forced to surrender in February 1943.

## Shoot-out

Germans and Soviets fought over every building in Stalingrad. Hand-to-hand fighting was widespread, and anyone showing himself was likely to be killed by sniper fire.

## Red Army cavalry

Red Army cavalry could move fast to the front line to support the infantry. Both sides used horses to tow supplies, but horses were easily bogged down by wet mud or snow in winter.

*Red Army cavalry brandish swords as they charge through the snow*

*T-34 was armed with an 85-mm gun after 1943*

## Tank superior

The Soviet T-34 tank, designed in 1939, was the mainstay of the Red Army armored units; 51,300 were built between 1941 and 1945 to carry a crew of five—one commander, two gunners, a loader, and a driver. With a speed of 32 mph (51 kph), the tank could cover 250 miles (400 km) without refueling. The slower German tanks were no match for them.

*Gun mounted in swiveling turret*

### EYEWITNESS

**The casualties**

About 91,000 German soldiers were captured at the end of the battle of Stalingrad, which saw both sides lose about 500,000 soldiers each. About two million Stalingrad civilians lost their lives. Amazingly, 10,000 civilians lived in the city throughout the battle and survived.

*T-34 diesel engine functions well in severe cold*

*Total weight 71,681 lb (32,514 kg)*

**Straw boots worn by German sentries in the Soviet Union**

## Frostbite

German soldiers fashioned snow boots out of straw to try to keep their feet warm and dry, as their stiff leather boots were too tight for layers of socks and too porous to keep out damp. Many suffered frostbite during Soviet winters.

*Wide tracks are ideal for crossing soft, uneven terrain*

# Inside the Soviet Union

Although the Soviet Union had spent two years getting ready for war, nothing could have prepared it for the suffering inflicted upon it—20 million Soviets died, and millions were enslaved by the Germans or killed in work camps. Yet civilians worked hard for victory and the war became known as the Great Patriotic War.

## Resistance fighters
Posters urged Soviets in German-occupied territory to join the partisans living in forests and "Beat the enemy mercilessly."

## Baltic states
The Baltic states (Lithuania, Latvia, and Estonia) were invaded by the Soviet Union in 1940 as part of the Nazi-Soviet pact and then again by Germany in 1941, before being taken back in 1944 by the Soviet Union. This 1944 Russian propaganda poster says "The Baltic states are free!"

Red Banner

Red Star

## Awards
The main medals awarded to Soviet soldiers were the Hero of the Soviet Union and the Orders of the Red Banner and the Red Star. Stalin also introduced the Orders of Kutuzov and Suvorov.

## Water, water everywhere ...
During the Soviet winter of 1941, the temperature in Leningrad fell to -40°F (-40°C). Food ran out and water supplies froze. People had to gather snow and ice to thaw.

Residents of Leningrad abandon their homes that were destroyed by Nazi bombs

## The Siege of Leningrad
The longest siege of the war took place in the Soviet city of Leningrad. German troops, supported by Finns, surrounded the city in September 1941. The Germans dropped more than 100,000 bombs and 200,000 shells, and killed 200,000 citizens, but failed to capture the city. The siege was eventually lifted by the Red Army in January 1944.

*Harvesting vegetables in a cathedral square, Leningrad*

## Feeding the city

During the Leningrad siege, every spare bit of ground was used to grow food, but rationing remained strict. More than 630,000 civilians died from starvation and the extreme cold.

*Mayakovsky Metro station in Moscow being used as an air-raid shelter*

## Attack on Moscow

Under attack from German troops in October 1941, many civilians sheltered in the Metro station. In December, the Soviets counterattacked and the German forces, suffering from low supplies and the harsh winter, pulled back.

**1942 poster urges Soviets to "Follow this worker's example, produce more for the front"**

## Produce more!

Despite this strong male image, more than half the Soviet workforce by the end of the war was female, playing a huge role in the defeat of Hitler by producing essential war equipment.

### The Molotov cocktail

Finnish troops in the Russo-Finnish War used "Molotov cocktail" gasoline bombs, named after the Soviet politician Vyacheslav Molotov.

## Snipers

Red Army snipers were engaged to shoot the enemy one by one. When a sniper achieved 40 kills, he was called "noble sniper."

**Soviet sniper rifle**

*Wooden handguard*

*Foresight*

## The Russo-Finnish war

After Germany invaded Poland in 1939, the Soviet Union tried to secure its western front and invaded Finland. The Finns fought back but, in March 1940, were forced to accept a peace treaty. The Soviets lost thousands more soldiers than the Finns, revealing Red Army weaknesses.

**Finnish Lahti 20-mm L39 antitank rifle**

*Wooden cheek rest*

*Rubber recoil pad*

# Desert fighting

In September 1940, Italy invaded Egypt from its colony of Libya, but the British overwhelmed the Italians. Italy's ally, Germany, sent troops to North Africa in February 1941, and a two-year desert battle was fought until the British 8th Army beat the German Afrika Korps at El Alamein in November 1942. US and British troops, landing in Morocco and Algeria, advanced east to surround the retreating Germans, forcing the Afrika Korps and their Italian allies to surrender in May 1943.

## Sly desert fox
Field Marshal Erwin Rommel (1891–1944), far left, commander of the German Afrika Korps, was known as the Desert Fox. He had the ability to quickly assess a situation and "sniff" out his enemy's weak points.

## Battle of Tobruk
The Mediterranean port of Tobruk, eastern Libya, was first held by the Italians, then captured by the British in early 1941, and then by the Germans in June 1942. The British recaptured it after El Alamein in November 1942. Pictured: a scene from the 1967 film *Tobruk*.

## El Alamein
The German Afrika Korps reached El Alamein by October 1942. This key coastal town was the gateway to Egypt and the Suez Canal (a shipping lane linking the Mediterranean to the Red Sea). Here, they met the British 8th Army and were defeated in a 12-day battle. The British victory marked a turning point in the war.

German antitank mine

British mine detector

## Mine alert
Vast minefields were laid around El Alamein by both sides, causing many deaths as tanks and infantry tried to navigate around them. A vast number still remain buried in the desert.

# Invasion of Italy's Sicily

The German defeat in North Africa opened the way for the Allies to invade Europe, but the Allies did not want to risk a direct attack against German forces. Instead, they invaded Italy, hoping to force it out of the war.

# Commonwealth help

Some units wore Arab-style cloth headwear to suit the hot African conditions. New Zealand units, including a Maori (native New Zealander) battalion, joined the British 8th Army.

*Cloth wrap kept out sand and sun*

## On the lookout in Libya

The German Afrika Korps, formed in 1941, used "donkey's ears binoculars" to view the enemy. It relied on Mediterranean convoys for reinforcements and supplies, which were attacked by the British.

## Well led

The British 8th Army was led by Field Marshal Montgomery. Monty's attention to detail and concern for troop morale led his army to victory at El Alamein.

## Monty's tank

Montgomery had his own tank, a US Grant M3A3, used for observation on battlefields and in the invasion of Sicily and Italy.

*Camouflaged in desert colors*

# Propaganda

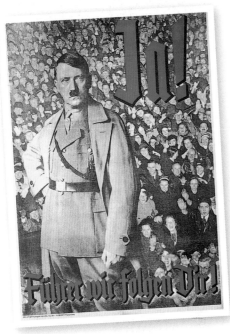

The war was fought with propaganda (spreading ideas) as much as ammunition, as both sides needed to convince their people that the war was right and that their side would win. Both sides manipulated public opinion to keep up morale and also used propaganda to break down enemy morale. Some propaganda was crude and some was subtle. Films, radio, leaflets, and posters were all used in the battle for hearts and minds, while entertainers traveled to sing to homesick troops.

## Hitler the leader

Propaganda did much to boost Hitler's image as a visionary leader, showing him surrounded by adoring followers, depicted as a great statesman who would achieve world domination.

## EYEWITNESS

### Tokyo Rose

Iva Toguri D'Aquino, known as Tokyo Rose, a sarcastic GI nickname, remains the only US citizen convicted of treason (sentenced to ten years in prison) before being pardoned. Trapped in Japan after Pearl Harbor, she worked on a Japanese radio show, which also broadcast anti-US propaganda.

British airmen load up with propaganda fliers

An umbrella caricatures the British soldier

## Bombarding the enemy with ideas

British and US bombers dropped six million leaflets over occupied Europe. Some warned civilians in occupied countries against cooperating with the enemy. Others told soldiers their efforts were futile and urged them to surrender.

Japanese insignia

German armband

## Kick out Brits

Italians wanted the Mediterranean to be an "Italian lake" and were attempting to kick the British out of North Africa. This 1942 Italian cartoon shows the Germans and the Japanese doing the same.

EUROPA

AFRICA

MEDITERRANEO

ASIA

## Allied power

Simple visual images were effective propaganda. This 1943 US poster shows the four Allied nations pulling apart the Nazi swastika. Constant reminders that the combined strength of the Allied nations could overcome the Axis did much to lift morale.

French Tricolor

British Union Jack

US Stars and Stripes

USSR Hammer and Sickle on Red Flag

## Poster wars

The British and Japanese governments engaged in a propaganda war in South Asia. This Japanese poster depicts Indian farmers being exploited by the British, while Winston Churchill enjoys his food dripping with blood.

## US war gods

A 1945 Chinese leaflet says this American pilot chased the Japanese out of the Chinese sky but needs help when hurt, lost, or hungry. It's telling rural Chinese which nations were friendly.

## Food as a weapon

The American government promoted food conservation and rationing, as well as growing one's own food—the Victory Garden campaign. President Franklin D. Roosevelt encouraged this practice and said in a speech that even small gardens helped. He emphasized that food was the "first essential" to winning the war. Posters like this one persuaded people to finish their leftovers.

LICK THE PLATTER CLEAN

Don't Waste FOOD

Food poster in the US, 1944

# The Holocaust

The Holocaust was the Nazi attempt to exterminate Europe's Jews. The Nazis were anti-Semitic (prejudiced against Jews), and sent Jews to concentration camps where many were worked to death. In the "Final Solution," they set up extermination camps to kill huge numbers of Jews each day. More than six million Jews were murdered.

### Anti-Jewish
This German poster advertises an exhibition called "The Eternal Jew." It was one way the Nazis spread anti-Semitic ideas. The Nazis boycotted Jewish businesses and passed the Nuremberg Laws, depriving Jews of their citizenship.

### First impressions
Many Jews sent by rail to camps thought they were off to work in Eastern Europe. Auschwitz concentration camp in Poland is preserved as a permanent reminder of the Holocaust.

### Warsaw ghetto
In 1940, Jews in the Polish capital, Warsaw, were herded into a walled ghetto. Conditions inside were awful and many died. In 1943, the Nazis attacked the ghetto to wipe it out. The Jews fought back; only 100 escaped.

*Jews are rounded up in the Warsaw ghetto at gunpoint*

### The yellow star
From 1942, Jews in German-occupied Europe had to wear a yellow star. This made it easier to identify them.

### Extermination camps
The Nazis set up concentration camps for Jews, communists, homosexuals, political prisoners, Romani, and other "undesirables." Eight extermination camps, notably Auschwitz (below) in Poland, had gas chambers to speed up the killing of Jews.

*Auschwitz Birkenau was the largest of the Nazi death camps*

*Stretchers were used to place bodies in the furnaces*

## Crematoria

The bodies of dead people were stripped of clothes, hair, jewelery, and gold teeth, and piled up for cremation. The crematoria were run by fellow prisoners, some of whom rebelled in Auschwitz.

## Camp conditions

Conditions were appalling. Food was scarce, workers endured 12-hour shifts, and many officers abused prisoners. Others conducted horrific experiments on both living and dead people.

## Feeding bowl

This empty tin, utilized by a prisoner, once contained cyanide gas crystals used in the gas chambers.

## Facing the truth

Allied troops marched local Germans into some camps to see the Nazi atrocities. As the camps were liberated by the Allied armies, the Holocaust horror became clear.

SS guards captured at Belsen

## Punishing the guards

For the Allied troops liberating the camps, the gruesome reality was too much to bear, and some shot the German SS guards. Some guards were made to bury the dead; some were put on trial for crimes against humanity.

# D-Day invasion

In the early morning of June 6, 1944 (D-Day), Operation Overlord—the Allied invasion of France—took place on Normandy beaches after years of planning. More than 150,000 US, British, and Canadian soldiers were ferried across the English Channel to establish five beachheads (shorelines captured from the enemy). The Germans were expecting an invasion farther to the east and had set up a defense there. By nightfall, the beachheads were secure. The liberation of German-occupied Europe had begun.

### Sky attack
Parachutists played an important role on D-Day. In the early hours, US Army paratroopers dropped behind "Utah" beach to secure vital positions. British paratroopers landed behind "Sword" beach and destroyed a German battery (gun site).

## Intelligent postcards
Allied intelligence used postcards of Normandy, plus maps, aerial photographs, and information from spies, to build up a picture of the coastline before invasion.

## "Sword" beach
This intelligence map details what the soldiers would encounter as they waded ashore. "Sword" (the most eastern beach), "Juno," and "Gold" were stormed by the British and Canadian forces; western "Omaha" and "Utah" by the US.

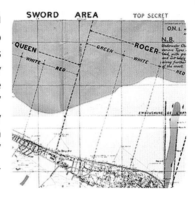

*Higgins boats had front ramps that allowed Allied troops to move ashore*

*800,000 soldiers crossed the Atlantic during the invasion, which was codenamed Operation Overlord*

## "Omaha" invasion
The most difficult landing site was "Omaha" beach, surrounded by high cliffs and with few routes inland. The US troops sustained 3,000 casualties but established a 2-mile- (3-km-) deep beachhead by nightfall.

## Mulberry harbors

"If we cannot capture a port we must take one with us," remarked a British officer. Two floating steel harbors (Mulberries) were built in Britain, towed across the Channel, and slotted together off "Gold" and "Omaha" beaches.

## Collapsible motorcycles

These were dropped behind enemy lines for landing airborne forces. The bikes had a range of 90 miles (144 km).

*Removable handlebar*

*Saddle-release mechanism*

*Gasoline engine*

**British Welbike motorcycle**

## On the beach

The day after D-Day, trucks, tanks, and troops flooded onto the beaches. The first wave of soldiers made each beach as safe as possible from enemy attack. Then ships unloaded vast amounts of equipment.

*Barrage balloons to protect supplies from overhead attacks*

*Mortar bomb ready to fire*

## Explosive work

The Allies pressed inland, encountering snipers, tanks, and fortifications hidden in the hedgerows. Progress was slow, but they soon had a million men in France.

# Liberation

Liberation from the Axis took a long time. The Red Army slowly pushed the Germans out of the USSR, but fighting continued in the Balkans into 1945. The Allied liberation of Italy from fascist rule was slow; liberation of France only began in June 1944. Denmark, Norway, and parts of Austria and the Netherlands were under Nazi rule until the Germans surrendered in May 1945. Only the Philippines, most of Burma, and some islands were recaptured from the Japanese by the end of the war.

## Fall of Berlin
On May 2 ,1945, two days after Hitler died by suicide, Soviet soldiers raised the Red Flag on top of the Reichstag (German parliament). It had taken two-and-a-half years to push the Germans back from Stalingrad to Berlin, the German capital.

## Liberation of Paris
The Germans occupied Paris from June 14, 1940. In August 1944, the Resistance rose up, Free French forces stormed the city, and the Germans surrendered. Free French leader, General de Gaulle, led a victory march (left).

## Battle for a free Italy
After the Allied liberation of Sicily in July 1943, Italy surrendered, changed sides, and declared war on Germany. German troops entered Italy, forcing the Allies to fight their way up the country, such as in the battle of Monte Cassino (below).

*Soldiers crawl over the rubble of the monastery at Monte Cassino*

Italian partisans in the liberation of Milan

## Freed from fascism
In April 1945, Allied forces entered northern Italy, helped by partisans of the Resistance Army. They fought to expel the Germans from Italy, to bring down the Italian government, and then to execute Mussolini.

## Denazification

With the Germans gone, local people removed all evidence of their former Nazi rulers. German-language signs and Nazi symbols were torn down as people began to rebuild their shattered countries.

## French freedom

The liberation of France was complete in early 1945. Nazi swastikas were ripped down and replaced with the French tricolor. The Free French, led by General de Gaulle, set up a government to take over from the Germans.

## EYEWITNESS

### Hidden identity

Maurice Kriegel-Valrimont was a communist and part of the French resistance. He was captured by the Germans but managed to escape and fought for the liberation of Paris. He is pictured (left) at the surrender of German General Dietrich Von Choltitz (right).

*Swastika surrounded by oak-leaf wreath*

The German national emblem (Hoheitsabzeichen)

## Hitler's eagle

This bronze eagle once hung in Hitler's official residence in Berlin. Captured by the Soviets during the final battle for Berlin, a Red Army officer gave it to a British soldier in 1946.

# The atomic bomb

Two German scientists split a uranium atom and caused a chain reaction of huge power in 1938. After the US entered the war in 1941, a team of scientists—many having fled Nazi Germany—turned this into a bomb. The Manhattan Project, based in Los Alamos, New Mexico, developed three bombs. The first was tested on July 16, 1945.

*Powerful twin-propeller engines enabled the B-29 to carry heavy loads over long distances*

### Enola Gay

This US Superfortress bomber dropped its load over Hiroshima, Japan, at 8:15 am on August 6, 1945.

*"Little Boy" was 10 ft (3 m) long with a diameter of 28 in (71 cm)*

### Small but deadly

The 9,000-lb (4,082-kg) bomb (named "Little Boy") dropped on Hiroshima was 2,000 times more powerful than any other bomb.

### Hiroshima horror

"Little Boy" exploded 2,000 ft (600 m) above Hiroshima. It created a blinding heat flash followed by a blast that flattened 5 sq miles (13 sq km) of buildings. Within five days, 138,661 people died.

**A Hiroshima survivor**

## "A shattering flash filled the sky ... and the world collapsed around me."

### Survivors

More than 200,000 citizens of Hiroshima and Nagasaki were killed by the bombs. Many more suffered burns and injuries such as radiation sickness. The long-term effects of radiation, including cancer, on survivors and their future children makes it impossible to calculate the exact number of deaths.

**Bottle fused by blast**

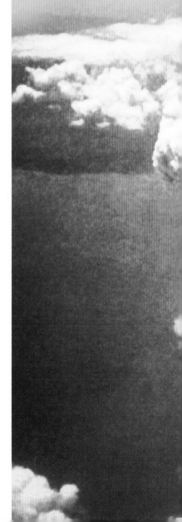

Mushroom cloud
visible 360 miles
(580 km) away

## Bombing of Nagasaki

On August 9, 1945, the final bomb was dropped on Nagasaki, Japan. "Fat Man" weighed 10,000 lb (4,536 kg). It was intended for Kokura, a military base, but poor weather meant Nagasaki was substituted at the last moment. About 73,884 people were killed.

Cloud rises
to 33,000 ft
(10,000 m)

## Japan surrenders

On the same day as the Nagasaki bombing, the USSR invaded Manchuria, Japan. Japan's Supreme War Council met with Emperor Hirohito, but came up with no plan. Hirohito took charge and, on August 14, surrendered to the Allies, provided he could remain as emperor. His broadcast to the Japanese nation was the first time they ever heard his voice.

*Japanese prisoners of war learn of their country's surrender*

### 👁 EYEWITNESS

**Burning memories**
Emiko Okada, one of the survivors of Hiroshima, was eight years old when tragedy struck. She was diagnosed with aplastic anemia years later. She said in an interview: "For three days and three nights, the city was burning. I hate sunsets. Even now, sunsets still remind me of the burning city."

Temperature at
ground level reaches
9,000°F (5,000°C)

# Victory

The Germans' unconditional surrender, on May 7, 1945, in Rheims, France, was witnessed by representatives from each major ally (Britain, the US, France, and the USSR). It was repeated in Berlin on May 8—VE (Victory in Europe) Day. After the two atomic bombs, Japan surrendered formally on USS *Missouri* in Tokyo Bay on September 2, 1945. After six years of war, the world was at last at peace.

### VE Day celebration
On May 8, the world could celebrate. Street parties were held across the US, Paris, and other newly-liberated European cities. In London, Prime Minister Winston Churchill appeared on the balcony of Buckingham Palace with the royal family to thousands of cheering people.

### George cross
First awarded by British king George VI in 1940 to those who showed heroism.

— *St. George killing the dragon*

**New York on VE Day**

### Front page news
British newspapers announced the end of the war. Prime Minister Winston Churchill said in his speech, "we may allow ourselves a brief period of rejoicing."

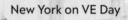

### Cross of Valor
Polish servicemen who displayed great courage in battle were awarded the Cross of Valor.

---

👁 **EYEWITNESS**

**VE Day in London**
English novelist Mollie Panter-Downes wrote in a letter that VE Day in London had the "quality of a vast, happy village fête ...." She described the day as an "immense holiday happiness" for the liberated people.

**Children celebrating VE Day in London, 1945**

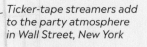
Ticker-tape streamers add to the party atmosphere in Wall Street, New York

## Fireworks over Moscow
Moscow celebrated with a fireworks display and military parade. Captured Nazi war trophies were laid at the Soviet leader's feet.

"East and west have met. This is the news for which the whole Allied world has been waiting. **The forces of liberation have joined hands.**"

—US Radio commentator, 1945

Indian newspaper printed in English

## Japan
VJ (Victory in Japan) Day, on August 15, 1945, was celebrated throughout the world, but many Japanese troops continued to fight. Peace was only finally established in September.

# The aftermath

## United Nations

Representatives of 26 nations met in Washington, D.C., on January 1, 1942, and agreed not to make peace with the Axis without the other UN members. A permanent UN organization was established in October 1945, with 51 members.

The world faced a huge task in 1945. Both sides suffered terrible losses with around 55 million deaths. The USSR lost 20 million people; Poland, one-fifth of its people; and six million Jews were killed. All countries, except the US, suffered ruined cities, factories, and farms. German and Japanese leaders were tried for war crimes, and their soldiers held in POW camps. In every country there was a strong desire never to relive the horrors of World War II.

### War crimes trials

Many Nazi and Japanese officials stood trial for war crimes. At Nuremberg, Germany, 1945–1946, a trial of 22 leading Nazis was organized by an International Military Tribunal; 12 were sentenced to death. In Japan, General Tojo was executed in 1948.

*Citizens cleared up their ruined towns and cities, and helped in the reconstruction*

### Affluent America

The US emerged stronger and richer than before the war. Except its Pacific islands, no part of the US had been bombed or invaded. Its people now entered a time of full employment and rising wages, and many could afford new homes and cars.

### Rubble gangs

A quarter of Germany's housing was destroyed in the war and had to be rebuilt. The work was very hard and unpleasant—they often found bodies in cellars and basements.

## Peace park

This memorial stands in Peace Memorial Park in Hiroshima, a reminder of the terrible damage nuclear weapons can inflict. Since the war, peace campaigners around the world have protested to ensure that nuclear weapons are never again used in war.

## Soviet control

The government of the Soviet Union wanted to retain control over the European countries it had occupied during the war. It imposed communist rule in Poland, Hungary, Romania, and others. This 1951 poster depicts the USSR and Czechoslovakia as friends.

## Two nations

1947 stamp of India

Britain lacked the resources to maintain large parts of its empire after the war. This led to the decolonization of many countries, such as India, which was divided into India and Pakistan in August 1947.

## Arab–Israeli conflict

With the British withdrawal from Palestine, the UN divided the territory into Jewish and Arab states. Thousands of Arabs had to flee the Jewish state of Israel in an exodus named "Nakba" (catastrophe). Refugees who are still in camps recall how their homes were bombed and razed to the ground.

## Prefab housing

Prefabricated (temporary) houses were built in postwar Britain to resolve the housing crisis. The prefabs came in kits and took a few days to construct. More than 150,000 were erected in the 1940s. Some still survive today.

# Did you **know?**

**A British soldier picks his demob shirt**

## BITE-SIZE FACTS

Some 29 amphibious Sherman tanks were launched from Allied ships on D-Day, but 27 sank in high seas. In 2000, divers located most of these tanks on the seabed.

In 1974, Japanese soldier Hiroo Onoda came out of the jungle of the Pacific island of Lubang after hiding there for 29 years, unaware that his country had surrendered.

Utility furniture was designed to use as little scarce raw materials as possible. It was available to newlyweds, or families who had lost everything in an air raid.

The charity Oxfam was set up in 1942 to raise money for children in war-ravaged Greece. Today, the organization helps relieve suffering all over the world.

In 2003, a message in a bottle washed up on a Swedish beach, sent 60 years earlier by an Estonian refugee hiding on Gotska Sandoen, 93 miles (150 km) away. Around 2,000 refugees from the Baltic states had found safety there in the war.

Where radio transmitters or telephones were unavailable, the military used carrier pigeons. Armies had special pigeon divisions with mobile pigeon lofts.

Japan and the USSR never formally ended hostilities. An official peace treaty in 2000 came to nothing. Japan wanted Russia to return four offshore islands that it seized at the end of the war.

In 1939, Swiss chemist Paul Müller realized the chemical DDT works as an insecticide. Thanks to his discovery, DDT protected troops from insect-borne diseases in the war.

**Princess Elizabeth (on the right)**

Princess Elizabeth, later the UK's Queen Elizabeth II, did her bit in the war. She joined the Auxiliary Territorial Service and drove a truck.

In 1935, the British government asked Robert Watson-Watt to work on a "death ray" to destroy enemy aircraft with radio waves. Instead, he used radio waves to detect incoming aircraft; radar (radio detection and ranging) was born.

On leaving the services, every British soldier received a set of civilian clothing: a "demob" suit, shirt, two shirt collars, a raincoat, hat, tie, two pairs of socks, and a pair of shoes.

Penicillin saved millions of soldiers' lives. It went into full-scale production in 1942.

Both sides used messenger dogs. The US army also trained platoons of war dogs. They served in the Pacific as scouts and sentries.

*Message brought by pigeon post*

**Members of the 8th Army Carrier Pigeon Service**

**A German soldier with his messenger dog**

# QUESTIONS AND ANSWERS

Sean Connery as 007 in the first Bond film, *Dr No* (1962)

### Which wartime double agent was the inspiration for James Bond?

Author Ian Fleming was impressed by Yugoslavian-born spy Dusko Popov, and based his character 007 on him. Abwehr (the German intelligence agency) recruited Popov in 1940, but he was anti-Nazi and soon spying for MI5 and MI6 (British intelligence agencies). They supplied him with fake information for his Nazi bosses. Popov spoke five languages, had his own invisible ink formula, and was the first spy to use microdots (photos shrunk to dot size). In 1941, he went to the US. He obtained intelligence that the Japanese were planning an air strike on Pearl Harbor, but the FBI did not act on this. In the US, Popov lived in a penthouse flat and went out with movie actresses, building a reputation for a playboy lifestyle. He wrote about his wartime activities in *Spy, Counterspy* (1974).

### What did Magic do in the war?

"Magic" was the codename for US cryptographers working on Japan's cipher "Purple Machine," invented by Jinsaburo Ito, in 1939. In September 1940, William Friedman cracked the code, leading to US success at the Battle of Midway.

### What secret code did American marines use?

From 1942, US Marines in the Pacific used the Navajo language as their secret code. It is a complex language and few non-Navajo could speak it. The Navajo had never needed military vocabulary, so existing words were given new meanings. About 400 Navajo, the Code Talkers, were trained to use the code. The Japanese never cracked it.

### Which side first used paratroopers?

The Soviets were the first, which they showed to military observers in 1935. They helped the Germans train their own. The Allies caught up only in 1940—the Central Landing School opened near Manchester, England. Soldiers from all of the Allied nations trained there and within six months, nearly 500 of them were ready for action.

**A paratrooper on an exercise**

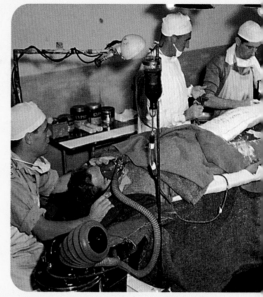

A soldier is given a blood transfusion at an advanced dressing station

### Which cutting-edge medical advance saved soldiers' lives?

The biggest life-saver was blood transfusion. Austrian-American doctor Karl Landsteiner had identified different blood types in 1901, but more work was needed. World War II was the first major conflict in which blood transfusions saved many lives.

### Which fighter planes had fangs?

The RAF painted shark's teeth on Curtiss Kittyhawks, which they flew in North Africa. The fangs raised morale by making the pilots feel invincible. The Kittyhawk could carry one 500-lb (227-kg) bomb and was armed with six 12.7-mm machine guns.

**Kittyhawks of No 112 Squadron RAF, 1943**

# Timeline

World War II was fought on many different fronts, and this timeline highlights some key moments to give a picture of wartime history as it happened. Unfortunately, there is not enough space here to list every major event of the war, so many milestones had to be left out.

German soldiers march into Poland, 1939

Japan attacks Pearl Harbor, 1941

## 1939

**September 1**
Germany invades Poland.

**September 3**
Britain and France declare war on Germany.

**September 27**
Polish Warsaw surrenders to Germany.

**September 28**
Germany and USSR divide up Poland.

**November 30**
The USSR invades Finland.

*Identification letters*

*Exhausts behind the propeller*

*Target symbol on wing.*

A Hawker Hurricane, used by the RAF in the Battle of Britain, 1940

## 1940

**April–May**
Germany invades Denmark, Norway, the Netherlands, Belgium, Luxembourg, France.

**May 26–June 4**
Operation Dynamo evacuates 338,000 Allied troops from Dunkirk, France.

**June 10**
Italy declares war on Britain and France.

**June 14**
German troops enter Paris, France.

**June 22**
France surrenders and Germany governs northern France.

**July 10**
The Battle of Britain begins.

**September 7**
Germany bombs British cities.

**September 13**
Italy invades Egypt.

**September 27**
The Axis sign the Tripartite Pact.

**October 12**
Battle of Britain ends.

## 1941

**January 22**
British and Australian troops capture Tobruk, Libya.

**March 1**
Bulgaria joins the Axis.

**April 6**
Germany invades Yugoslavia and Greece.

**May 27**
The British sink the *Bismarck*.

**June 22**
Germany invades the USSR.

**September 15**
The Siege of Leningrad begins.

**December 7**
Japan attacks Pearl Harbor and starts to invade Malaya.

**December 8**
Britain and the US declare war on Japan.

**December 11**
Germany declares war on the US.

**December 25**
Hong Kong surrenders to the Japanese.

The Germans in North Africa, 1942

## 1942

**February 15**
The Japanese capture Singapore.

**March**
First prisoners at Auschwitz, Poland, are gassed.

**April 28–May 8**
The US halt Japanese advance at the Battle of Coral Sea.

**June 4–6**
The US defeat the Japanese at the Battle of Midway.

**August 19**
The battle for the Soviet city of Stalingrad begins.

**October 23–November 4**
Britain defeats Germany at El Alamein, North Africa.

**November 8**
US and British troops land in northwest Africa.

## 1943

**January 31**
The German army is defeated at Stalingrad.

**February 8**
The US captures Guadalcanal from the Japanese.

**April 19**
Nazi troops attack the Warsaw ghetto in Poland.

**May 12**
The German army in North Africa surrenders.

**July 9**
Allied troops invade Sicily, Italy.

**July 25**
Benito Mussolini is overthrown.

**September 3**
Allied troops invade mainland Italy. As a result, Italy surrenders.

**October 13**
Italy declares war on Germany.

## 1944

**January 27**
The Siege of Leningrad ends.

**March 8**
Japan attempts an invasion of India.

**June 6**
D-Day: Allied forces land in Normandy, France, and press inland.

Benito Mussolini

**August 25**
The Allies liberate Paris.

**October 20**
US troops land in the Philippines.

## 1945

**March 7**
British and US troops cross the Rhine River, Germany.

**April 30**
Adolf Hitler dies by suicide.

**May 7**
Germany unconditionally surrenders.

**May 8**
VE (Victory in Europe) Day.

**August 6**
The US drops "Little Boy" atomic bomb on Hiroshima, Japan.

**August 9**
The US drops "Fat Man" atomic bomb on Nagasaki, Japan.

**August 15**
VJ (Victory in Japan) Day, following Japan's surrender.

**October 24**
United Nations (UN) is founded.

US troops in the Philippines, 1944

# Find out more

You may be able to hear about the war first-hand from older generations of your family. Personal accounts are also online and in books. Many war museums have interactive displays that bring wartime to life and TV documentaries show footage of the war. Finally, movies have dramatized almost every wartime experience.

### Cabinet War Rooms

In London, you can visit the underground Cabinet War Rooms where Prime Minister Churchill and his War Cabinet met from 1940 until the end of the war. The rooms are just as they were during the war.

### Monument at Murmansk

Every country that was in World War II has memorials that remember the dead, such as this concrete statue of a Soviet soldier, known as "Aloysha," which symbolizes the USSR's war heroes.

### D-Day anniversary

Anniversaries of wartime events, such as D-Day, are a chance to reflect and find out more about your country's history.

### War museums

World War II collections in museums are still expanding, as more artifacts come to light. The Imperial War Museum North in Manchester, UK, displays a large collection.

Imperial War Museum North

## War films

Films express not only the horrors of war, but also stories of individual bravery. *Schindler's List* (1993) dramatizes the true story of a German businessman, Oskar Schindler, who saved hundreds of Jews by employing them in his factory.

Film poster of *Schindler's List*

*The menorah is an important symbol of Judaism*

## Holocaust memorial

Many memorials honor those who died in Nazi death camps. This memorial at Mauthausen, Austria, is shaped like a *menorah* (candlestick).

## Caught on film

One of the most gripping tales of the resistance is the 1964 film, *The Train*. French railroad worker Labiche tries to sabotage a Nazi train smuggling art out of Paris before liberation.

## USEFUL WEBSITES

- Online collection of the Imperial War Museum
  **www.iwm.org.uk**
- Multimedia site with an area on children's experiences
  **www.bbc.co.uk/history/worldwars/wwtwo**
- A multimedia resource about the Holocaust
  **www.history.com/topics/world-war-ii/the-holocaust**

## Omaha beach D-Day memorial

The inscription reads: "The Allied forces landing on this shore, which they call Omaha Beach, liberate Europe—June 6th 1944."

## PLACES TO VISIT

**PEARL HARBOR, HAWAII**
- USS *Arizona* Memorial
- USS Battleship *Missouri* Memorial

**WASHINGTON, D.C.**
- Holocaust Museum
- WWII Memorial

**JAPANESE AMERICAN INTERNMENT MUSEUM, ARKANSAS**
- "Against Their Will" exhibit relating to the internment of Japanese American citizens during WWII

**HMS BELFAST, LONDON, UK**
- Royal Navy cruiser that was active in the war, now kept as a museum

**IMPERIAL WAR MUSEUM, LONDON, UK**
- Walk-through "Blitz Experience" and Permanent Holocaust exhibition

**JERSEY WAR TUNNELS, ST. LAWRENCE, JERSEY, CHANNEL ISLANDS**
- Exhibits tell the story of the German occupation of the Channel Islands

**LE MÉMORIAL DE CAEN, FRANCE**
- Interactive displays and archive films
- Affiliated tours of the D-Day beaches

**MUSÉE DE LA RÉSISTANCE, GRENOBLE, FRANCE**
- Documents relating to the activities of the French Resistance

**ANNE FRANK HOUSE, AMSTERDAM, NETHERLANDS**
- Exhibition of Jewish wartime diarist Anne Frank's life
- The Secret Annex where the Frank family hid from the Nazis

*English translation of the French inscription, which appears above*

# Glossary

**Air raid** A bomb attack from the air.

**Air-raid shelter** A place that afforded protection from the bombing during an air raid.

**Alliance** A group of allies who have agreed to act in cooperation; they often set out shared aims in an official treaty.

**Ammunition** Bullets and shells.

**Amphibious** Operate on land and water

**Antiaircraft gun** A gun with enough range to fire at enemy aircraft.

**Anti-Semitic** Holding views that discriminate against and persecute Jews.

German airmen making ammunition belts

**Armistice** End of hostilities.

**Atomic bomb** A powerful weapon that uses nuclear fission—the splitting of an atom from a radioactive element.

**Atrocity** An appalling, wicked act.

**Auxiliary** Describes someone providing help or backup.

**Axis** The name of the alliance of Germany, Italy, and their allies.

**Barrage balloon** A tethered balloon, strung with cables, used to obstruct low-flying aircraft.

**Blood transfusion** Injecting blood from a donor into the veins of a patient who is losing blood.

**Bunker** An underground bomb shelter.

**Camouflage** Coloring and patterns designed to blend in with the background.

**Cipher** A code that substitutes letters or symbols by a set key.

**Communist** A supporter of Communism—a belief system that opposes the free market and aims for a classless society.

**Concentration camp** A prison camp for nonmilitary prisoners. At Nazi concentration camps, prisoners included Jews, Eastern Europeans, and other groups considered to be enemies of the state.

**Convoy** Merchant ships traveling together, protected by a naval escort.

**Cryptographer** Someone who studies, creates, or deciphers codes.

**Cryptography** The study and creation of secret codes.

**Demobilization** Dispersing troops after active service.

**Democratic** Based on the principles of democracy, where government representatives are elected by the people.

**Dictator** A ruler who takes total control, without giving the people a say.

**Espionage** Spying.

**Evacuate** Move away from danger.

**Evacuee** Someone who has been removed from a place of danger.

**Fascist** A supporter of fascism—a belief system opposed to democracy and in favor of a powerful, armed state.

Locating a target for an antiaircraft gun

A Gurkha in jungle camouflage, Malaya

**Field telephone** A portable military telephone.

**Fuselage** The body of an airplane.

**Gas** In the context of war, a poisonous gas used to harm or kill the enemy. All sides had supplies in World War II, but it was never deployed as a battlefield weapon.

**Gas chamber** An enclosure where people were murdered using gas.

**Gas mask** A breathing device that gives protection from a gas attack.

**Gestapo** Nazi secret police service.

Field telephone

**Ghetto** An area of a city where a particular racial group are confined.

**Grenade** A small bomb that is hurled by hand.

**Holocaust** The mass murder of millions of Jews and others by the Nazis during World War II.

**Imperial** To do with an empire or emperor.

**Incendiary** Describes a bomb, bullet, or other device designed to cause fire.

**Infantry** Foot soldiers.

**Intelligence** Useful military or political information, or the spies who gather it.

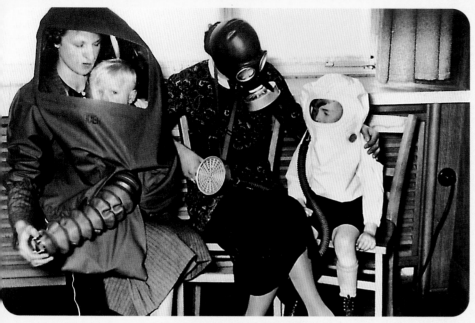
German gas mask designs, 1939

**Land girl** A young woman who worked to help the war effort, usually on farms to produce food. Women were also put to work producing other valuable resources, from raw materials to weaponry and parachutes.

**Liberation** Freeing from occupation.

**Machine gun** An automatic gun that fires bullets in rapid succession.

**Mine** (1) An underground chamber packed with explosives.
(2) A bomb laid below the surface of the ground that detonates when traveled over.
(3) A floating bomb in the sea for destroying ships and submarines.

**Minesweeper** A ship that drags the water to find undersea mines.

Young women working at a sawmill

**Morale** Strength of purpose, confidence, or faith.

**Morse code** A code where each letter of the alphabet is represented by dots and dashes.

**Mortar bomb** A heavy bomb, usually fired from a tank.

**Nationalist** Someone who believes in nationalism—the belief in the importance and dominance of their own nation state.

**Occupation** An enemy force taking over a country.

**Paratrooper** A soldier air-dropped into territory, wearing a parachute.

**Partisan** A member of a resistance movement working in enemy-occupied territory.

**Penicillin** A mold extract that prevents bacteria growth. Its antibacterial properties were discovered by Alexander Fleming in 1928. By 1942, penicillin was available to treat soldiers with infections.

**POW** "Prisoner of War." Someone captured in wartime. Mostly members of the armed forces.

**Propaganda** Information intended to convince people of a particular viewpoint. It could be posters, broadcasts, or air-dropped leaflets, for example.

**Radar** "Radio Detection and Ranging." A detection system that uses radio waves to locate objects.

**Radiation sickness** Illness caused by exposure to radioactivity.

**Rationing** Restricting provisions, such as food, in a time of scarcity.

**Refugee** Someone forced to flee their country in search of safety.

**Resistance** An organization opposed to an occupying enemy force, especially the European groups that sabotaged the Nazis during their occupation of Europe.

**Sabotage** A deliberate action designed to destroy or disrupt.

**Shell** An explosive device that is fired, for example, from a cannon.

**Surrender** Give up control.

**Swastika** An ancient symbol—a cross with each arm bent at a right angle—adopted by the Nazis as their emblem.

**Torpedo** A self-propelled underwater missile, fired from a boat or submarine.

**Treaty** A formal agreement between nations.

**U-boat** A German submarine.

Alexander Fleming with a Petri dish of penicillin

**Ultimatum** A final demand which, if it is not met, will result in serious consequences and a total breakdown of communication.

**Utility** Describes clothing, household objects, or furniture produced in wartime Britain under the Utility Scheme. All Utility items were designed to waste as little as possible, in terms of both raw materials and the manufacturing process.

# Index

# Acknowledgments

The publisher would like to thank the following people for their help with making the book: Terry Charman, Mark Seaman, Mark Pindelski, Elizabeth Bowers, Neil Young, Christopher Dowling, Nigel Steel, Mike Hibberd, Alan Jeffreys, Paul Cornish, and the photography archive team at the Imperial War Museum for their help; Simon Holland and Ashwin Khurana for editorial assistance; Sheila Collins for design assistance; Samantha Nunn, Marie Osborne, Amanda Russell, Surya Sankash Sarangi, and Pushp Vagisha for additional picture research; the author for assisting with revisions; David Ball, Neville Graham, Rose Horridge, Joanne Little, and Susan Nicholson for the wallchart; BCP, Marianne Petrou, and Owen Peyton Jones for checking the digitized files; Saloni Singh, Priyanka Sharma-Saddi, and Rakesh Sharma for the jacket; Vijay Kandwal for DTP assistance; and Joanna Penning for proofreading and indexing.

The publisher would like to thank the following for their kind permission to reproduce their photographs:
(Key: a-above; b-below/bottom; c-centre; f-far; l-left; r-right; t-top)

4 Dorling Kindersley: Imperial War Museum, London / Andy Crawford / By kind permission of The Trustees of the Imperial War Museum, London (tl); Dorling Kindersley: Geoff Dann / Imperial War Museum, London (cl). 5 Alamy Stock Photo: PA Images / Tim Ireland (bc). 6 Alamy Stock Photo: Maurice Savage (tr). Peter Newark's Military Pictures: (bl). 6–7 Alamy Stock Photo: Glasshouse Images / JT Vintage (c). 7 Getty Images: Universal Images Group / Universal History Archive (tr). 8 Getty Images: Hulton Archive / Keystone (bc). Hulton Archive/Getty Images: (cl, cla). Peter Newark's Military Pictures: (tl). 8–9 Alamy Stock Photo: Shawshots (b). 9 Alamy Stock Photo: Chronicle (tr); Sueddeutsche Zeitung Photo / Scherl (l). TopFoto.co.uk: (br). Weimar Archive: (tc). 10 Hulton Archive/Getty Images: (cl). 11 Getty Images: Hulton Archive / Fred Morley (l). Peter Newark's Military Pictures: (tr). 12 The Ronald Grant Archive: British Lion Films: (b). Hulton Archive/Getty Images: Keystone (tr). 12–13 Alamy Stock Photo: (b). 13 Alamy Stock Photo: Süddeutsche Zeitung Photo (tr). akg-images: German Press Photo (tc). 14 Hulton Archive/Getty Images: Keystone (b). 15 Hulton Archive/Getty Images: Keystone (tr). 16 Bridgeman Images: (cra). Hulton Archive/Getty Images: (b). 16–17 Getty Images: Hulton Archive / Keystone (b). 17 Dorling Kindersley: H Keith Melton Collection (br). 17 Hulton Archive/Getty Images: (c). Getty Images: Popperfoto (tc). 18 Alamy Stock Photo: World History Archive (br). Peter Newark's Military Pictures: (c). 18–19 Alamy Stock Photo: Shawshots (c). 21 Bridgeman Images: Picture Alliance (c); Max Mumby / Indigo (cra); ullstein bild Dtl. (br). 20 Corbis: Hulton Deutsch Collections (clb). Hulton Archive/Getty Images: Fox Photos (bc). 20–21 The Ronald Grant Archive.

22 Alamy Stock Photo: INTERFOTO / History (tl). Getty Images: Mondadori Portfolio (c). 22 Peter Newark's Military Pictures: (cra). 22–23 Mary Evans Picture Library: (c)Robert Hunt Library (b). 23 Alamy Stock Photo: Phil Crow (tr). Dorling Kindersley: Eden Camp Museum, Yorkshire (cb). Getty Images: Imperial War Museums / Fg. Off. Forward (cl). Imperial War Museum (tl). 24 Alamy Stock Photo: CPA Media Pte Ltd / Pictures From History (c). Hulton Archive/Getty Images: (bl). 24–25 Alamy Stock Photo: Shawshots (c). 25 Imperial War Museum: B5501 (tr). Hulton Archive/Getty Images: Keystone (tc). Peter Newark's Military Pictures: (cb). 26 Dorling Kindersley: H Keith Melton Collection (cra, crb/cover, crb). Hulton Archive/Getty Images: (crb). Peter Newark's Military Pictures: (cl). Royal Air Force Museum, Hendon: (cla). 27 Alamy Stock Photo: PA Images / Anthony Devlin (clb); Northcliffe Collection / ANL (bc). 28 Alamy Stock Photo: David Cooper (cb). Hulton Archive/Getty Images: Keystone Features (clb). 28–29 Getty Images: Hulton Archive / Keystone (cla). 29 Alamy Stock Photo: PA Images / Tim Ireland (tl). Shutterstock.com: CT / Bournemouth News (cra); Northcliffe Collection / ANL (bc). TopFoto.co.uk: (br). popperfoto.com: (br). 30 Alamy Stock Photo: Pictorial Press Ltd (cra). 31 Dorling Kindersley: H Keith Melton Collection (tl); H Keith Melton Collection (cl). Getty Images: Hulton Deutsch Collections (tr). Peter Newark's Military Pictures: (br). Shutterstock.com: (cra). 32 Library of Congress, Washington, D.C.: LC-DIG-fsa-8d34277 / Feininger Andreas (tr). Peter Newark's Military Pictures: (clb). 33 Alamy Stock Photo: Alpha Historica (tc). Dorling Kindersley: Imperial War Museum, London / Andy Crawford / By kind permission of The Trustees of the Imperial War Museum, London (tl). Corbis: (cra). 34–35 Imperial War Museum. 34 Bridgeman Images: © Look and Learn (bc). Getty Images: Imperial War Museums / No 9 Army Film & Photographic Unit (br). Imperial War Museum. Peter Newark's Military Pictures: (tl). 35 Alamy Stock Photo: Granger Historical Picture Archive, NYC (br). Getty Images: Imperial War Museums / Ministry of Information Official Photographer (cra). popperfoto.com: (br). 36 Dorling Kindersley: Eden Camp Museum (clb). Peter Newark's Military Pictures: (tl). 36–37 Alamy Stock Photo: Shawshots (t). 37 Getty Images: Universal Images Group / Sovfoto (cb). Imperial War Museum (cr). Peter Newark's Military Pictures: (b). 38 Alamy Stock Photo: Niday Picture Library (c). Hulton Archive/Getty Images: (b). 39 Alamy Stock Photo: Marc Tielemans (cla). Getty Images: Corbis Historical (br). Hulton Archive/Getty Images: (bl). 40 Getty Images: Corbis Historical (b). 41 Getty Images: Imperial War Museums / No 9 Army Film & Photographic Unit (cl); Popperfoto (cra). Peter Newark's Military Pictures: (b). TopFoto.co.uk: (cla); Press Association (b). 42 Alamy Stock Photo: charistoone-images (cra). 42–43 Alamy Stock Photo: INTERFOTO / History (ca). 43 Hulton Archive/Getty Images: (tc). TopFoto.co.uk: (crb). 44 Imperial War Museum: RUS2109 (tr). 45 Alamy

Stock Photo: SPUTNIK (t). akg-images: (cra). Imperial War Museum: (cr). 46 Alamy Stock Photo: Pictorial Press Ltd (cl). Getty Images: TASS (bl); Universal Images Group / Sovfoto (cr). 47 Alamy Stock Photo: SPUTNIK (tl, cla). Dorling Kindersley: Ministry of Defence Pattern Room, Nottingham (b). Peter Newark's Military Pictures: (tr). 48 Alamy Stock Photo: mccool (bl). TopFoto.co.uk: (tr). 48–49 Alamy Stock Photo: Everett Collection Inc (clb). TopFoto.co.uk: (tl, tr). 50 Getty Images: Mondadori Portfolio (b). Alamy Stock Photo: Hi-Story (clb). Getty Images: Corbis Historical / swim ink 2 llc (br). Shutterstock.com: Everett Collection (t). Peter Newark's Military Pictures: (b). TopFoto.co.uk: (cl). 51 akg-images: (t). 52 Peter Newark's Military Pictures: (bl). TopFoto.co.uk: (c, tr). 52–53 Corbis: Carmen Redondo (t). 53 Camera Press (t). Corbis: Hulton Deutsch Collections (c). Hulton Archive/Getty Images: US Army Signal Corps Photograph (cr). TopFoto.co.uk: (br). 54 Getty Images: Bettmann (tr); Royal Geographical Society (with IBG) / Sir John Edgell (ca). 54–55 Alamy Stock Photo: Shawshots (b). 55 Dorling Kindersley: Royal Signals Museum, Blandford Camp, Dorset (t). The US National Archives and Records Administration: Department of Transportation. U.S. Coast Guard. Office of Public and International Affairs. 4 / 1 / 1967-1985 (c). Peter Newark's Military Pictures: (cr). 56 Alamy Stock Photo: Everett Collection Inc (crb). Getty Images: Gamma-Rapho / Keystone-France (c). Peter Newark's Military Pictures: (bl). 56–57 Alamy Stock Photo: Shawshots (t). 57 Getty Images: Roger Viollet (bc). Hulton Archive/Getty Images: (cb, c). 58 Alamy Stock Photo: Prisma by Dukas Presseagentur GmbH / Schultz Reinhard (bl). 58–59 Science Photo Library: US National Archives and Records Administration (c). 59 Getty Images: The Washington Post / Mitsu Maeda (tr). Peter Newark's Military Pictures: (tr). Corbis: (cr). 60 Alamy Stock Photo: CBW (cl); Chronicle (bc). Dorling Kindersley: Eden Camp Modern History Theme Museum, Malton (cb). 60–61 Corbis: Bettmann. 61 Hulton Archive/Getty Images: Alexander Ustinov (c). 62 Corbis: Hulton Deutsch Collections (br). The Advertising Archives: (clb). TopFoto.co.uk: (br). 62–63 Alamy Stock Photo: Ivan Marchuk (c). 63 Alamy Stock Photo: CPA Media Pte Ltd / Pictures From History (crb); Kay Roxby (c). Getty Images: Corbis Historical / Michael Nicholson (tr); Hulton Archive / Keystone Features (br). 64 Alamy Stock Photo: mauritius images GmbH / United Archives (br). Getty Images: Hulton Archive / Central Press (c). Imperial War Museum: (bl, tr). 65 Imperial War Museum: (tr, cr, b). Rex / Shutterstock: United Artists (tl). 66 Hulton Archive/Getty Images: Fox Photos (cb). Corbis: Bettmann (cra). 67 Imperial War Museum. Corbis: Bettmann (tr). 68 Corbis: Richard Klune (b); Yogi, Inc. (cr); Sygma / Orban Thierry (c). TopFoto.co.uk: Universal Pictorial Press (b). 68–69 Hulton Archive/Getty Images: Fox Photos. 69 Corbis: Owen Franken (br); Michael St. Maur Sheil (ca). Rex / Shutterstock: Amblin/Universal (tl); United Artists (cl). 70 Dorling Kindersley. Imperial War Museum: (tr, cr, bc). Getty Images: Hulton Archive: Chronicle (ca); IanDagnall Computing (crb). Getty Images: Imperial War Museums (bl).

All other images © Dorling Kindersley
For further information see: www.dkimages.com